THE QUEEN'S CLOAK

To Mother
with love,
your first born!

THE QUEEN'S CLOAK

A Myth for Mid-Life

JOAN CHAMBERLAIN ENGELSMAN

CHIRON PUBLICATIONS
WILMETTE, ILLINOIS

Fourth Printing, 1996

Library of Congress Catalog Card Number: 93-15576

Printed in the United State of America
Editing and book design by Siobhan Drummond.
Cover design by D. J. Hyde.

Library of Congress Cataloging–in–Publication Data:
Engelsman, Joan Chamberlain, 1932-
    The Queen's cloak : a myth for mid-life / Joan Chamberlain Engelsman.
        p.   cm.
    Includes bibliographical references (p.) and index.
    ISBN 0-933029-73-X : $14.95
    1. Middle aged women—Psychology. 2. Middle age—Psychological aspects. I. Title.
    HQ1059.4.E64 1993
  305.24'4—dc20   93-15576
                                      CIP

ISBN 0–933029–73–X

IN MEMORY OF MY MOTHER

CONTENTS

ACKNOWLEDGMENTS

"The Queen's Cloak" has been a work in progress for a long time and there are many people I would like to thank. First and foremost is my husband, Ralph, who has "listened me into being" more times than I can count. His support and enthusiastic encouragement make all the difference in my life, and his good-natured acceptance of my telling tales about him in this book is deeply appreciated. My loving thanks also goes to my sons, Marc and Dan, to Kim and Sue, the wonderful women they married, and to my grandchildren, Robby, Josh, and Anna, who fill me with hope and delight. I cannot conclude these family thoughts without remembering my father, who died this past year. His pride in me, as well as his poems and puns, helped shape my life. The next tale's for you. This one, as you have already noticed, is for my mother.

Many women have helped bring this story to its final form. In the beginning there was Merrill Skaggs, teacher, author, scholar, dean, and Gail Andersen Myers, friend and author. Carol Smith, Lydia Masterson, Marilynn Anderson, and Carol Hornbeck, who actually read the entire book in two incarnations, have been wonderfully helpful with their comments and enthusiasm. So also have been my students at Drew University and Princeton Theological Seminary, my colleagues and friends at Womanspace, and the many women who have participated in discussions and workshops with me. I have learned from them, borrowed many of their stories, and am deeply grateful to them and others who have shared my journey.

Several other people have touched and changed my life. I can't imagine how I could have written this book without Shirley Sugerman—analyst, friend, and wise woman first-class.

Janet Fishburn and Gabriel Coless have been wonderful theological colleagues, teachers, and companionable friends. And Viv Leopold and Susanrachel Balber help keep me all together.

Finally, I would like to thank Murray Stein, for loving the fairy tale and suggesting the commentary in the first place; Fredrica Halligan for inviting me to share part of this work at the Fires of Desire conference at Fordham in April 1991; Siobhan Drummond, my editor at Chiron Publications, for understanding what it's all about, and Marlene Raedisch for her perceptive drawings.

THE QUEEN'S CLOAK

 nce upon a time, after the winter festival, the Queen realized she was bored and rather depressed. Looking at her ladies-in-waiting, she asked if anyone could think of something interesting to do. Most suggested the same old things, but one woman remembered that long ago the Queen had mentioned doing an inventory of the castle.

"Now is the time," cried the Queen with delight, because doing something seemed better than doing nothing. During the weeks that followed, the women searched every nook and cranny. They set down what they found in long lists.

One day the Queen and her maid were working in the attic when they came upon a group of boxes and trunks which had belonged to the Queen's mother. They had been delivered after she died. Some had been opened, but most had been put away untouched.

Now the Queen went through them all. The last to be opened was the smallest. Inside the little trunk was a beautiful cloak made of different threads and colors. It was woven in an intricate design that made the cloak seem to shimmer.

The Queen had never seen it before. As she lifted it out of the chest, she was surprised, but pleased, when a note fell to the floor. Written in her mother's hand, the letter was addressed to the Queen.

My Dearest Daughter:

This is a cloak I wove myself. Take what you need and give the rest to your sister. A wise woman will be able to tell you about its magic. This is my greatest legacy. I leave it to you with my love.

The Queen was shocked. She had not known her mother had a magic cloak, and now she did not understand the message. But she gathered the soft folds in her arms and carried it back to her apartment.

In the days that followed, she tried on the cloak many times. It was too short, and really too small. The strangest thing was the way it changed. Although the cloak looked beautiful hanging in the wardrobe, every time the Queen draped it over her own shoulders the colors faded and the pattern disappeared.

As for the magic, no one could understand it. The Queen uttered every magical phrase she had ever heard, but nothing happened.

One day, the Queen told her maid to put the cloak away because the mystery was too much for her.

"Have you sought the help of the wise woman?" asked the maid.

"No," said the Queen. "I didn't know there was one in the kingdom."

"Oh, yes. She lives in a little house at the edge of the wood."

"If you know her, will you ask her to come to the castle and explain everything to me."

"I will do my best," said the maid.

Several days later, she told the Queen that the wise woman could not come to the castle. On the other hand, if the Queen wanted to come to the cottage, she would be happy to see her.

The next day, the Queen and her maid set out in the royal carriage. When they got to the edge of the woods, the Queen followed the directions given by her maid and walked to the wise woman's house.

Rap, rap, rap, went the Queen against the door. Then she opened it and went inside. The wise old woman sat by the fire sorting seeds.

"Are you the wise woman? Well, I am the Queen. My mother said someone like you might help me."

Before the woman could reply, the Queen told her the whole story. When she finished, the cottage returned to silence—broken only by the crackling of the fire and the pounding of the Queen's heart.

Finally the wise woman spoke.

"The magic and the cloak belonged to your mother. I cannot tell you how to use it. But if you want, I can tell you how to make a similar cape for yourself."

"Oh, yes," said the Queen, as she clapped her hands in excitement. "I have always wanted to do magic."

"Very well," replied the wise woman. "But it is quite difficult and sometimes dangerous. First, the linen and wool you need you must make and dye yourself. So you must plant your own flax and spin your own wool. Next, you must take yarn from something you made for every member of your family. You will also need to add some material from your mother's cloak. Finally, you must get something from a stranger."

"When you have collected all the right materials, you must weave it yourself in your own pattern. Once you have begun, you have only a year to finish it, and you cannot tell anyone what you are doing or why, otherwise there will be no magic."

"That is ridiculous," said the Queen, stamping her foot. "I can't possibly do all those things myself. Besides, I don't need a magic cloak. I am the Queen."

Then she turned her back on the wise woman and started to leave the cottage.

"If you change your mind, your maid can advise you about some things. And I will help you if I can," said the wise woman gently.

By the time the Queen got home, she was more depressed than ever. What was the point of being a Queen if you had to work like a servant? And how could she take back anything she had made for her husband and children? Maybe if she could tell them what it was all about—but she could never do it if she had to keep her reasons to herself.

For two days and nights, she didn't eat or sleep. She argued with herself. She really could not believe her mother had ever undertaken such a project. She could not imagine herself doing it. It was much too difficult.

On the third day, she saw a face in the mirror. It was sad and frightened. With a shock, the Queen knew it was her own, and she began to cry for herself. After weeping a long time, the Queen stood up and called her maid.

"I have decided to make my own cloak. It will be very hard, but the wise woman said you could help me. Will you do that?"

"Gladly," said the maid. "First let me draw you a bath and get you some food. Then we can plan."

Since spring was just beginning, the Queen decided to start by planting flax. She selected a field far away from the castle so no one would see her. Then her maid arranged to have a farmer plow it.

On the appointed day, the Queen and her maid rode forth as though for pleasure. When they reached the field, however, the work began. The Queen dug and planted while the maid held the tender shoots, handing them one by one to her mistress.

Within an hour the Queen could do no more. Filthy and aching in every bone, she could barely hang on to the horse for the ride home.

"What happened to you?" said the King.

"I fell off my horse."

"That's too bad," he said. "Do be more careful."

Had anyone ridden by on the following day, they would have been surprised to see their Queen (was it their Queen?) in bare feet and an old maid's dress bent over the rows.

So it went. The trip to the field, the change of clothes, the digging and planting, the painful ride home.

This is how the field was planted—with salt from tears and sweat, and blood from blistered hands and feet. But on the day it was finished, the Queen laughed. Running to her horse, she brought out a picnic she had hidden in her saddle. Like a pair of conspirators, she and her maid celebrated together.

This part was easy, thought the Queen. Now I have to take back something I gave my husband and children. The Queen knew they would be angry, because no one likes to give up something they think is theirs. She wished she could take something surreptitiously, but the wise woman said she had to tell them face to face.

First the Queen spoke to her husband. I hope my voice doesn't quaver and I don't loose my nerve, she thought.

"Good husband, do you remember your coronation robe which I embroidered with gold thread?"

"Oh, indeed. I was very young, but that robe made me look and feel like a king. I really showed everybody, didn't I?"

The Queen coughed. "Yes, dear. But now I need to pick out the gold thread for another project."

"That's terrible. If you take out the gold thread, the robe will look like any other robe. No one will know I'm a king."

"That's silly," said the Queen with a smile. "The robe does not make you a king. You were born to your position and have your own power and authority."

"Oh, that's right," said the King with a sigh of relief. "Besides, I think it's time for a new one. The weavers guild has pestered me to wear something they have made. I think I'll have a design contest. It will be good for business."

So while the King planned his new wardrobe, the Queen picked out the gold thread, rolled it into a ball, and set it aside.

Next the Queen went to her son. Hanging on the wall was a small tapestry on which she had woven her family's coat of arms.

"I have come to take down the small tapestry I made you," she said. "I need the material for a new project."

"But mother, if you take it away, I will not have a kingdom of my own."

"My son, that is not yours. You know that if you have ambitions to be a king, you have to find your own realm."

"Oh, that's right," said her son with a grin. "Besides, I don't like your country. I'd much rather go adventuring with my friends and find something new."

So while the Prince and his friends planned their travels, the Queen unraveled the tapestry, rolled the colored threads into balls, and put them away.

Finally, she went to see her daughter. "My dear," she said nervously, "do you remember the afghan I made you when you were little? I need to take it back because I want the yarn for another project."

"Oh, Mama. I love it so. It reminds me of how you used to nurse me. I still snuggle in it on rainy days. Someday when I'm married and have my own children, I plan to give it to my daughter."

Dear me, thought the Queen, this is harder than anything.

"I am happy it means so much to you. But now you are old enough to care for yourself. If you want, I can teach you how to make something of your own."

"Would you, Mama? That would be wonderful. I'd really like to make something in a different color, and a little bigger. Besides, I saw another pattern I liked better."

So while the Princess planned all the new things she was going to make, the Queen unraveled the afghan, rolled the wool into a ball, and put it away.

After the Queen had collected something she had made from every member of her family, she took out her mother's cloak. Carefully she cut it in half from neck to hem. She quickly took apart one half and set it aside for her own cape. After deftly catching the threads along the edge of the other piece, she wrapped it so it could be sent to her sister.

"Half and half. I think that's fair, don't you?" said the Queen, making a face. "I'll ask the next traveler to take it along to her kingdom."

Now that the Queen had finished many of her tasks, she decided she should talk to the wise woman. This time, she rode her horse. It was easier than getting out the royal carriage.

Tap, tap, tap, went the Queen. Suddenly she was feeling very shy, so she waited a long time at the door until she felt brave enough to enter. The wise woman was sitting by the fire shelling nuts.

"How is everything going?" she asked. The Queen told her about planting the flax, about getting something she had made from every member of her family, and about dividing her mother's cloak.

"That is very good," said the wise woman. "But what have you taken back from your sister?"

"From my sister? Nothing," said the Queen angrily. "She is a terrible person. I have neither seen nor spoken to her since before I was married. I have not made her anything."

"Not even when you were young?"

The Queen started to answer as before when suddenly she remembered. "Oh, no! When I was fourteen, I made her a shawl to look like the starry heavens. I can't ask her for that. She would kill me."

"If you do not get it back, you cannot make your cloak."

"And you are a mean and stupid old woman," cried the Queen. "Even if I did that, how could I get something from a stranger when I don't know any?"

The Queen slammed the door as she left and galloped her horse all the way home.

In the days that followed, the Queen's anger abated, but it was replaced by fear. Fear of her sister, fear of the journey, fear of the unknown. The only thing the Queen had to encourage her were the balls of thread she had already collected, the calluses on her hands, and the calm presence of her maid.

One day, the Queen rode out to the field of flax. Looking down at the rows, she realized all the pain and labor she had already known would be meaningless unless she asked her sister for the shawl. So she resolved to go.

The Queen's decision to visit her sister threw the castle into a frenzy of preparation. Her family was shocked, but she allayed their suspicions by telling them she felt obliged to deliver a package entrusted to her by their dead mother.

Early one summer day, when all was ready, the Queen left for her sister's kingdom. She was dressed in beautiful clothes and rode a white horse. Her trunks were filled with fine clothes and jewelry and lovely presents. All these were packed on a mule which followed the royal horse.

In her excitement, the Queen forgot her sister's piece of the cloak. But the maid remembered, and she tucked the package among the many boxes on the mule.

As long as the procession wended its way through the Queen's realm, she was guarded by her husband's soldiers. When she crossed into her sister's kingdom, however, she was alone. As she rode along, leading the mule, her fear returned.

Not long afterward, a man appeared from the woods. He barred the way with his sword and ordered the Queen off her horse. Pushing her to the side of the road, he pawed through the rich gifts. When he saw the remnant from her mother's cloak, he laughed.

"Give me your clothes. You can wrap yourself in this old rag."

As soon as she was naked, he looked at her and laughed again.

"You are a dried–up old stick, aren't you."

Then the man gathered up all her belongings, took her horse and mule, and disappeared as quietly as he had come.

As fear and humiliation overcame her, she wept bitter tears.

Since there was nothing to do but continue, she finally dragged the piece of cloak around her. She was as sad and forlorn a figure as any who ever trudged along the road.

It was evening when she reached the castle.

"Who are you?" demanded the gatekeeper.

Drawing herself up as best she could, the woman said, "I am the Queen's sister. Please take me to her."

Sick and exhausted, the woman did not notice the bright lights and music that filled the castle. Nor did she see all the people who stopped to stare at her.

When she was ushered into the great hall, she only had eyes for her sister. Gathering her last strength, the woman removed the remnant of their mother's cloak. Standing naked, she offered it to her sister.

At that moment, she collapsed.

In the days that followed, the woman struggled between life and death. When her eyes could focus again, she saw her sister sitting beside her.

"So, you have decided to live. Good, I am glad."

The woman's heart began to pound until she realized she had nothing to fear. She was lying in a fine bed, the people in the room seemed ready to help her. Furthermore, her sister was smiling.

"We thought you might die. But we put our resources at your disposal, and now you have recovered."

"You do not hate me?" said the woman.

"Not at all," said her sister. "But since you always wanted to kill me, I have wondered why you came and what is the meaning of this piece of cloth."

"It is from our mother's magic cloak. She entrusted it to me. Now I have given you half, according to her wishes."

The woman lay back on the pillow.

"Why did the gatekeeper let me in?"

"We were having a masquerade, and he thought you were a guest dressing as a beggar."

"That's almost right," said the woman. And the two sisters laughed.

Under the care of her sister, the woman grew strong. They had time for many talks and grew to know each other as never before.

As the summer drew to a close, the woman made plans to return to her own kingdom.

Her sister gave her many presents, but the woman refused them.

"This time I will travel lightly."

"What can I give you to commemorate our reunion then?"

"Many years ago, I made you a shawl that resembled the starry night. Now I have need of it. If you will give me that, I will be grateful."

"It is yours," said her sister.

And when the woman left, they parted sweetly.

"Let me ride with you to the border."

"No," said the woman. "This time I am simply dressed with nothing but a mule. I do not think anyone will bother me."

When the sun was high overhead, the Queen decided to rest for awhile. She was hot and sweaty by the time she reached a small lake she remembered seeing before.

This will be a perfect place to stop, she thought. I can even refresh myself with a swim. So the Queen led her mule to a secluded spot, took off her clothes, and slipped into the water.

While she was relaxing, she noticed a man coming down to the lake from the other side. The woman concealed herself from view, but continued to watch.

Like herself, the man took off his clothes and went for a swim. Then, gracefully, he stretched himself out on a rock to bask in the sun.

The sight of the man made her heart pound. Then, slowly, heat began to spread through her loins.

Hardly aware of what she was doing, she began to glide through the water toward the rock. By the time he saw her, however, the woman had resolved her mind. She stood in the lake and held out her hand.

The man gazed in appreciation; then he rose to meet her.

They played together until both were content. Then the woman went back to the water.

"I don't know you," said the man.

"No, you don't," said the woman, who suddenly started to laugh.

"Will you give me something to remember this day?" she said.

"What would you like?"

"Your stockings would be perfect."

So the man picked them up, waded out into the lake, and tied them around her waist.

"I will need nothing to remember you," he said with a smile.

Then she swam off to the other side of the lake.

After she got home, the Queen unraveled her sister's shawl and the woodsman's stockings, rolled up the yarn into balls, and put them away.

Fall came quickly, and the Queen harvested the flax and spun the wool. Under her maid's direction, the Queen worked with an easy mind. She did not tire as easily as she had in the spring. In fact, she came to like the work.

While she was making the yarn, the Queen began to imagine what the cloak might look like. She wanted it to be impressive, and rather elegant. Being a Queen was not easy. Wearing a magic cloak would certainly come in handy, she thought, especially when she was feeling overwhelmed.

When the Queen had made and collected all the yarn she needed, she knew the time had come to design the pattern.

Her mind was full of many images: the straight rows of flax; the reflections of the spinning wheel on the floor; the vee that spread out behind her when she swam in the lake; the curving path that led to the wise woman's door.

The Queen tried to remember the pattern in her mother's cloak. I wish I had not unraveled it so quickly, she thought. But she did recall patches of blue from the piece she clutched to her body as she stumbled to her sister's castle. I do not have any blue, she thought, except for a few strands, so I will dye the flax that color in memory of her.

Then she set out all the balls of yarn. Not only did she need to make a pattern, she had to decide what colors to use where. The more she thought about this project, the harder it became. As she planned, she tried to imagine how it would appear to others.

Will it look regal? Will it make me look strong, she thought? What is the best style? How can I work in all the patterns and colors?

As the days grew shorter, the Queen became more upset. No one could help her, and she began to feel that all her work had been in vain.

One day, she sat down on the floor and placed the balls of yarn around her. As she stared at them, she noticed the red and black had rolled together.

I really don't like them together, she thought. So she moved the red ball. Then she moved a gold one.

From where I sit, she thought, some colors seem more complimentary than others. And so she moved the balls around her. While she did, she held them in her hand, gathering in her lap those she was unsure about until she found the perfect place.

That afternoon, she played until she knew all the shades and textures of her yarn. Finally the Queen had them spread about her in a way that pleased her. Even the colors she didn't like had found a place.

Then she stood up in the middle of them. At that moment, she knew how to design her cloak. The cloak flows out from me, she thought. The colors and patterns will only look right when they come out from the center. "Which is me," she said out loud with a smile and a tremble.

In the days that followed, the Queen worked out her design. Carefully she balanced the patterns, mindful of the final effect but attending to her own preference.

Finally the Queen and her maid set up the loom. As the Queen began to weave, she started to sing. They had a merry time, and soon everyone in the castle found reasons to come to the Queen's apartments. Even the king, who came more than most.

At last everything was accomplished. The Queen's cloak fell in soft, radiant folds from her shoulders to the floor. It had a deep hood which she could wear as a collar or pull up over her head.

When she walked, the cloak moved about her gracefully while the light played off the gold and silver threads. The intricate pattern showed the various colors to their advantage.

"Now it is time to go back to see the wise woman," said the Queen.

So one fine day, she wrapped up her cloak and walked to the cottage at the edge of the wood.

Knock, knock, knock, went the Queen at the door. When she entered, she found the wise woman stringing garlands.

"I have come to show you my cloak," said the Queen, as she draped it over her shoulders.

"Do you want me to tell you about the magic?"

"No," said the Queen. "I understand. It is not in the cloak. That is why you could not tell me. It comes from making the cloak."

"Yes," said the wise woman as she stood up, "I see you have become a wise woman yourself."

The two women laughed and embraced. They spent the day enjoying each other's company, stringing garlands for the winter festival, and eating and drinking cakes and wine.

The night of the great festival, the Queen wore the cloak for the first time. Although it was very beautiful, most people didn't even notice it. Instead they saw the Queen—which is as it should be.

And the Queen used her wisdom like magic to bring peace and healing to the land.

INTRODUCTION

I

When I was a young girl, I loved fairy tales and myths. Old ones, new ones, Greek, German, Arabic—it made no difference to me, I read them all. Of course, the ones with pictures were the best. So were the movies made from the stories. But what I liked most was acting them out.

Apparently, my friends did too. One of them had a large front porch which we turned into a stage. Our costumes were made of borrowed finery and crepe paper, the colors of which ran in the rain. I'm fairly sure we reenacted "Snow White and the Seven Dwarfs," with myself as a brown crepe papered dwarf. I also remember a red cloak made of similar material, but my most elegant attire was a long blue dress, accessorized with a tinsel crown and a stick with a star on the end.

These happy memories slipped to the back of my mind long ago, but they must have prepared the way for my appreciation of these stories as an adult. By the time I rediscovered them, the characters and situations were being taken seriously by anthropologists, psychoanalysts, and professors of religion, who saw them as symbols of the personal and societal psyche and as representatives of the divine. To find my childhood treasures respected put me in what a friend of mine from Texas calls "hog heaven."

Since that time, I have derived great pleasure from working with myths and symbols. The gods and goddesses of various religious traditions have enriched my theological understanding, while the images and events of legends and fairy tales have been a rich storehouse of information about human nature. I have even used the various elements of these tales as a basis for personal reflection on my own life.

Knowing that I appreciate this material so much, it probably should not be surprising that I would use this format to tell a story. But I was quite startled when, some time ago, an afternoon's reverie produced the major ingredients of "The Queen's Cloak." My first thought was to use the queen, her sister, the magic cloak, and all the other characters as the basis of a novel, but every attempt was a disaster. After a number of false starts, I abandoned the project as much too difficult.

Several years later, I introduced a new graduate course on mothers and daughters in myth, legend, and fairy tale. It was an unusual undertaking in many ways, having no syllabus and few lectures, but requiring the students to present three short papers on various aspects of the mother–daughter relationship. The students were scholarly but also so creative that eventually I decided to contribute something in a similar vein.

Suddenly I remembered "The Queen's Cloak." This time, I knew how to write it, and four days later the major ingredients had assembled themselves into a fairy tale which I could share with my students. We examined it the same way we had explored all the other myths and fairy tales—we looked at the sociological, psychological, and spiritual aspects of the story. I was very gratified to find "The Queen's Cloak" meant something to them because, as we worked with the material, I felt the characters and situations certainly had something to say to me.

In the years since that class, I have shared this story with many other students, friends, and analysts, who did not think it odd to scrutinize a fairy tale to find meaning for adult women. It is their observations, as well as my own reflections, which form the core of this commentary.

One way to work with "The Queen's Cloak" is to let it provide a general structure for meditating on your life. There are several major themes in the story which illustrate various issues arising for women at mid-life. One of the most important concerns is the mother–daughter relationship. Although the mother never actually appears in the story, her spirit hovers in the background.

As the fairy tale progresses, we follow the queen as she interacts with her mother's cloak, first wanting this, then wanting that piece of material. Each season reveals a different aspect of this struggle, aspects many of us experience as our mothers age and die. Becoming mother to one's mother and living through the trauma of her death trigger many memories. Reviewing the queen's struggle may help focus your own reflections.

There are various other issues which can also arise at mid-life. Many of us seek to reclaim options, aspirations, and dreams we put on hold when we were younger. New possibilities, which were not imagined before, can suddenly appear and draw us toward them. And powerful emotions, once disavowed or repressed, may suddenly clamor for recognition. These obstacles are some of the challenges we share with the queen as she struggles to make her cloak.

Finally, as we mature, we come to appreciate the sense of urgency which is part of "The Queen's Cloak." When I was young, my grandmother would often comment on how fast time flies: "The older I get, the quicker it goes." Now that I'm no longer a child, I understand. In the fairy tale, the queen has only a year to gather all her material and design her cloak. In reality, we may have more time than that, but by mid-life we know it is limited.

Because of this, many of us feel keenly that it is now or never to "get ourselves together" or to "find out what we want to do when we grow up." We wear so many hats, symbolic of the different roles, demands, and expectations facing us, that we often feel exhausted or paralyzed by indecision.

Once I saw a cartoon that captures this situation perfectly. A man and a woman are sitting on a couch in front of the TV. In a bubble over the man's head, two thoughts are pictured—beer and a football. In the bubble over the woman's head are sixteen different images depicting parts of her life, such as her children, aging parents with their medical bills, her job, the household (cooking and housework), her husband, *and* a football. All are whirling around her head as she sits folding laundry.

When I first attempted to reconcile the conflicting demands in my life, I turned to the Rule of St. Benedict to see if its triune focus on work, study, and prayer could help organize my life. Slowly, I learned the solution was not simply a question of better time management with certain percentages given to family, career, friends, public causes, and reflection.

It was not until I wrote "The Queen's Cloak" that I realized the queen's final struggle was my own. Having it all is not the same thing as getting it all together. Her life is full of options, demands, talents, and feelings competing for energy and attention; but while she concentrates on them, she cannot make her cloak. Faced with this impasse, she stumbles onto a solution. By reorienting her self—beginning at the center—she discovers the deep core of her being. After that, everything falls into place.

How can this happen? In my opinion, this profound change in the queen's life is based both on her earlier efforts to recollect herself, as well as on making contact with the deep self which emerges from within. This self, which is the queen, is also a unique fragment of the divine. The self is truly the queen, but it is also truly divine.

Christians celebrate this mystery as the dual nature of Jesus. Buddhists talk about the Buddha nature which lives within everyone and strives to be released. Other religions use other language, but the queen recognizes this astonishing combination in her hidden self and her trembling expresses her awe at what lies within and beyond her.

Because I have written this fairy tale, I have to ask myself if I can do as well as the queen. I believe her discovery is the right key, but in real life it remains an ongoing struggle. Nevertheless, reflecting on her experience does help me refocus; it calls me back to my self.

In other times and cultures, this kind of centering practice has been associated with religious experience. Meditation, chanting, even dancing have been used to bring one who seeks into contact with the divine. In my opinion, the self the queen discovers has this connection to the divine.

The fruits of her yearlong struggle bear witness to the enormous changes in her life. After making her cloak, she reconnects with others in such positive ways that her family and friends want to be with her. Her relationship to both maid and wise woman becomes that of companionable equals, and she reaches out to bring peace and justice to unknown others.

The contrast between her life before and after the cloak is great. Before, the queen was passive, depressed, arrogant, selfish, and obsessed with her own needs. Later, she becomes happy, active, loving, focused, and inclusive in her interests.

There is no doubt that the queen's resolution is idealized. In reality, I don't know whether anyone comes close to living out a fictionalized story like this. But I believe it is personally, culturally, psychologically, and spiritually accurate; therefore, the queen's quest encourages me to continue on my own.

II

If you are interested in deliberating on some of the themes from "The Queen's Cloak," the following suggestions may be helpful. Some of them derive from comments and observations made by students and friends who have enjoyed thinking about the tale; some from my own experiences.

When I was working on my symposium paper, "Women and the Rule of St. Benedict," I discovered that most women I interviewed took some time each day for reflection. These quiet times often came at odd hours. Some rose at 6 A.M. to have a quiet cup of coffee before starting the day. Others set aside time late at night after everyone had gone to bed. Shower time or just before sleep were also popular moments to review the day.

If you have a similar practice, you may want to devote some of your meditative time to various episodes or moments in "The Queen's Cloak." Taking off from the story, you can use the themes as focus points for thinking about your own life. You can also use them as a way to direct your own fantasies. A lot of us daydream or fantasize; some of us even feel guilty about it. Yet imagination is a wonderful asset for living a full life.

There is no substitute for this personal pondering, but you might also enjoy sharing "The Queen's Cloak" with some of your women friends and then reflecting on it together. Years ago, I was part of a group which met once a month. Some of us were thinking about going back to school, others about going to work, two were considering divorce. We starting meeting together quite spontaneously; fifteen months later, equally abruptly, we stopped. During that time, all of us were trying to juggle many different things, but through the group we were able to support each other in a variety of ways. We also learned from each other. When we disbanded the group, it was because we were ready to move on to something else. In a similar vein, you might find it interesting to use episodes in "The Queen's Cloak" to spark a discussion with your friends.

Like physical exercises, these are psychological exercises that can be done over and over. We never know ourselves perfectly; we can only hope to know ourselves better. In the fairy tale, as in life, the magic is in the making of the cloak, not in the garment itself. The cloak is only the outward and visible sign of a process which takes place within. Thus, although I wrote "The Queen's Cloak" many years ago, I still review the queen's tasks to aid my reflections on my life.

Although the fairy tale can help focus attention on some specific areas and help us contemplate some of the sociological, psychological, and spiritual factors in our lives, it is not a substitute for psychotherapy. Working with a trained professional is very different from exploring one's self alone. Sometimes the former is necessary in order to get on with the latter.

There are various episodes in "The Queen's Cloak" which can bring up material you may want to talk through with a therapist. This may be particularly true in the scene with the thief. Because of my work at Womanspace, Inc., educating clergy about the prevalence of family violence and helping them set up programs which will lead to peace in the home, I am unhappily familiar with violence against women and children. Whether it is spouse abuse, child abuse, date rape, or child sexual abuse, thousands of women and girls suffer violence in their homes every day.

Living with violence or in psychological fear or bondage to another person is a terrible thing. Every state has laws to protect such people, and most large communities have professionals who can shelter women and children and save lives. They can certainly help empower women to live better ones.

For women who were physically or sexually abused as a child, *The Courage to Heal* can be a wonderful book friend. "The Queen's Cloak" may be able to sensitize them to what is happening or has happened in their lives, but it is *not* a substitute for working with a trained professional helper.

If considering various episodes of this fairy tale awakens past memories or encourages you to challenge a present situation that is harmful, I hope you will find a shelter worker, therapist, social worker, pastoral counselor, or clergy man or woman who will stand with you as you struggle forward.

The points of reflection, which make up the major part of this commentary, direct our attention to several areas. First, they highlight some of the toxic effects of the cultural roles and stereotypes which contribute to women being strangers to themselves. For example, the queen explores several qualities, such as her anger and her sexuality, that society usually denies women.

Most of us are brought up on "princess" stories—tales usually dominated by a wicked stepmother who persecutes the girl, and a fairy godmother and charming prince who save her. Little is expected of the princess except to do as she's told. This emphasis on goodness and obedience may have been appropriate for young girls a hundred years ago, but today we would probably select other virtues. Certainly, as adult women we need to cultivate different qualities in order to gain the different desires and hopes we have now. "The Queen's Cloak" may help you pinpoint some of the material you need.

This fairy tale also works on other levels. Years ago, my children had a three-dimensional tic-tac-toe game. There were four planes with sixteen squares on each plane. It was hard to play and took great concentration because of the number of ways a player could score on any level or by going up, down, or diagonally through the various planes.

Although this image is far from exact, it creates an interesting visual picture of the multiple aspects of our lives. As in the game, we live on many levels at once. Sometimes the result is harmonious. Occasionally we are at odds with ourselves, but usually we concentrate on one or two levels and forget the other planes altogether. Yet because they continue to play a role in our lives, the ignored levels can be a source of surprise and confusion.

The psychological and spiritual planes, which intersect family and society, are the ones most commonly overlooked. This is certainly the case with the queen who, although caring of others, is quite out of touch with her own needs and desires. Correcting this imbalance becomes one of her major tasks, and much of her effort is focused on these levels.

As you go through the commentary, you will find that some of the characters and situations prod the queen to look inward. Others encourage her to consider, and reconsider, her relationships with others. Various episodes work on many levels at once. But the culmination of all these efforts comes when she must bring all the threads together in one design. Either she has come to know herself on every plane or she will fail.

I recently enrolled in an art class to learn to draw portraits. I have a certain knack for detail, but my teacher keeps coming over and saying, "No, no! That's not a face. It has no structure. You must build it from inside." Then she undoes everything and tells me to concentrate on the bones and the planes of the face. The details, she assures me, come last. After several months, I'm finally beginning to grasp what she means by building the picture from within.

The purpose of the queen's effort is similar—to understand herself from within, to feel more and more centered in her self and less and less controlled by the peripheral details of her life. Because this is the opposite of what most women have been taught, many of the queen's labors are directed toward undoing what she learned. This reorientation is one of the primary tasks of mid-life.

In "The Queen's Cloak" we get to see the queen change from a bored, depressed, passive person who relies on others into an active, self-confident, joyful woman. The episodes discussed in the rest of this commentary are some of the critical ones in her transformation. I have intentionally included a variety of things to consider. Please do not restrict yourself to these incidents—others may speak more eloquently to your own life. These are just some of the ones my friends and I have found provocative or helpful.

WINTER

I

*Once upon a time, after the winter festival,
the Queen realized she was bored and rather
depressed. Looking at her ladies-in-waiting,
she asked if anyone could think of something
interesting to do.*

Getting started can be the hardest, or the easiest, part of any
project. For example, when it comes to handiwork, I'm a first-
class starter. Although I have bags full of unfinished sweaters,
quilts, and afghans, I always find it hard to resist a new and
beautiful pattern. On the other hand, when it comes to my life,
I often find reasons to postpone time for reflection, in other
words, *not* to start. Usually, I let the press of current events take
precedence.

Many of my friends have shared similar observations
about themselves. Now they wonder why the queen suddenly
decides to look inside herself—which is what the inventory is
all about.

There are several reasons which might motivate us to
consider or reconsider our lives. The most obvious cause is usually a trauma of some kind. The death of our mother, husband,
child, or close friend can trigger a felt need to examine our own
existence.

Our children can also provide a major source of shock.
The sudden discovery that a son or daughter is using drugs,
had a mental breakdown, attempted suicide, is homosexual,
has run away or been arrested can be motivation enough. After
the initial crisis is over, many of us will look within if only to
determine "what we did wrong." At least, this has been the
case for many women who have lived through such events.

Fortunately, what begins as an act of self-recrimination may often turn into a more realistic voyage of self-discovery. This is certainly true for a woman I know whose daughter suddenly attempted suicide. After successful intervention and the beginning of treatment, my friend launched an attack upon herself. She blamed herself for her child's unhappiness. Only gradually could she let go of her culturally conditioned guilt and begin to evaluate her own life.

Life-changing crises provoke many of us into embarking on a voyage of personal discovery. Going through a divorce is probably number one on this list. Moving (particularly if it wasn't your idea) or losing a job are also significantly upsetting events. Even positive changes—such as starting a job, having a baby, going back to school—can provoke a reevaluation of one's self.

It is relatively easy to understand why crises and traumas would motivate us to look at ourselves, but there are other, more subtle causes which can also move us. It's amazing how relentless simple things can be. A sense of aimlessness, of vague irrelevancy, a wish that life could be "better," can become a constant source of irritation which, like water on a rock, eventually erodes our façade.

The queen's boredom and depression belong to this latter category. These feelings probably hide a host of other, far less acceptable ones the queen would like to cover up. Certainly, as her adventure unfolds, we can see there is a wide range of emotions which appear to be unfamiliar guests in her heart.

Many of us are like the queen—at least to some extent—and her reasons are more than ample to start her reflecting on her life.

Whatever the motivation may be, one formidable obstacle confronts the queen before she can begin: her passivity. There are few things more dangerous to our health than this habit which is often drilled into us from birth. General inertia causes enough trouble, but women must surmount an additional obstacle. When it comes to the most important matters of life, most of us have been conditioned to wait.

We wait for men to ask us out, and we wait for them to propose marriage. We wait for a raise. We often wait for others to suggest something to do, whether in an emergency or for an evening out. I once heard a respected college professor remark, without challenge, that he had never been at a dinner party where a woman initiated a topic of conversation.

Like the queen in her passivity, we rely on others to tell us what we want, even what we feel. Because we have been so conditioned to avoid the initiative, we come to rely on others to read our minds. Telling them what we want is not only difficult, it becomes undesirable: "If I have to tell him what I want for my birthday, it won't be the same."

We have expectations, but they remain unspoken. Even Lois Lane, crack reporter, sings a poignant song. While flying with Superman, she whispers to herself words many of us may have said: "If you want to be loved, come to me. Read my mind."

Sometimes our lack of initiative is merely regrettable, but in its extreme form, this behavior can be life-threatening. I recently heard a night nurse on a cancer floor talk about a woman who called her at the hospital. She had gone into crisis but was reluctant to wake her doctor, even to save her own life.

Every woman struggles with this problem in one way or another. We have been conditioned by society to expect men to lead and to wait for them to do it. Those of us who refuse to accept the stereotype are often called pushy, uncooperative, or butch. Unfortunately, these negative images are so powerful they can still turn a ten- or eleven-year-old dynamo into a passive, fifteen-year-old girl. Sad to say, by the time we are mature, our psyches are full of ladies-in-waiting who counsel us to do the same old thing. Therefore, in order to begin her transformation, the queen has to hear the one small voice that remembers other possibilities.

If we listen carefully, we can hear that voice in us.

*One day the Queen and her maid were
working in the attic when they came upon a
group of boxes and trunks which had
belonged to the Queen's mother. They had
been delivered after she died. Some had been
opened, but most had been put away
untouched.*

One of the most important ongoing themes in "The Queen's
Cloak" is the bond between mother and daughter. Aspects of
their relationship play an important role in every season, just as
they do in our lives. Unfortunately, this powerful influence is
rarely considered in all its complexity. Like the queen, most of
us settle for superficiality, setting aside any profound aspects of
our kinship for another day.

That day arrives when we decide to do a personal inventory. Suddenly we discover a forgotten legacy which, in my
opinion, holds the most important key to our centered self. When
the queen finds her mother's things, she finds the cloak with its
instructions. Without this gift, she would have returned to her
ladies-in-waiting still looking for something to do. But once the
queen opens the smallest trunk, her life is irrevocably changed.

Most of us are not willing or able to open that little trunk
until we reach the middle of our lives. By the time we mature,
certain things have begun to nudge our psyches into an awareness of the mother–daughter bond. My women friends describe
these in different terms, but they all have a certain similarity.

As we get older many of us find our mothers within. "I
looked in the mirror and saw my mother." "I suddenly heard
myself sounding just like her." "I was at a meeting the other
day and found myself responding just like she does." Often
these unconscious affinities make us very uncomfortable. One

woman friend cut her hair because she could no longer distinguish herself in the mirror. "All I could see was Mom and I hated it."

Whether or not we are upset by these unsolicited echoes of our mothers in our lives, these intrusions mark her strong return to our consciousness. If you live in the same community as your mother, you may be aware of the closeness of your relationship; but if you moved away or your mother is no longer alive, these flashes of memory serve as strong reminders.

In addition to unbidden comparisons, many of us quite consciously begin looking for similarities with our mothers. Some seek a role model. Others want her help and support. An oft-quoted anecdote about a young man may explain the reason for our own renewed interest. According to the story, when the boy was fourteen, he thought his father was a fool. When he turned twenty-one, he was amazed to discover how much his father had learned in seven years.

Finding out how much our mothers have learned since we were teenage girls is a gift of mid-life. We go to her for advice, for sympathy. We call her when our children are sick, when they give us trouble, when they're getting married. If she had a good marriage, we ask for her secrets as well as her recipes. She is usually the strongest female presence in our lives, and as a woman we are profoundly shaped by her influence.

This reality is never clearer than when she dies. My mother died six summers ago, and I was stunned by the depth of my grief. Nothing in the culture, in my studies, or in my work prepared me for this experience. Male psychoanalysts frequently discuss the significance of their father's death. More than one describes it as *the most important event in a son's life*. Unfortunately, I don't know any therapist who has said the same thing about the impact of a mother's death on her daughter.

In the years since my mother's death, I have talked about this phenomenon with countless women who have lived through the same experience. Whether privately or in class, most of them seem relieved when I bring it up. When I indicate I am prepared to take their feelings seriously, their responses are amazing.

The word most frequently used to describe the sense of loss they feel is *devastating*. Years after the event, many women will start to cry when they talk about their mother's death. Students have left the room in tears, only to return and share their feelings. One day, I mentioned this to a friend, who confessed she was still unable to drive by the house where her mother died seven years before. Even when a former neighbor invited her to drop by, my friend declined because she didn't think she could survive the trip emotionally.

As part of my lectures and workshops on the queen's quest, we talk about the death of our mothers. One day, a woman laughed and said that what I was calling a mid-life crisis had started for her when she was twenty-seven. Suddenly, while the others were still chuckling, she got a strange look on her face. "That was two years after my mother died," she said. And everyone stopped laughing.

Whether through death, unexpected flashbacks, or conscious attachment, our mid-life struggles seem to be strongly related to a return to our mothers. As the queen discovers, we have unfinished business here.

In the days that followed, she tried on the
cloak many times. It was too short, and really
too small. The strangest thing was the way it
changed. Although the cloak looked beautiful
hanging in the wardrobe, every time the
Queen draped it over her own shoulders the
colors faded and the pattern disappeared.
    As for the magic, no one could
understand it. The Queen uttered every
magical phrase she had ever heard, but
nothing happened.
    One day, the Queen told her maid to
put the cloak away because the mystery was
too much for her.

Reconnecting with her mother, the queen suddenly reexperiences herself as the child who used to play dress up. Once her mother's clothes were too big. Now they are too small. And when she wraps her mother's cloak around herself, trying to imitate her mother, the queen must watch all the lovely glitter and shine fade away.

Although the queen eventually abandons this game, she still clings to the idea that her mother has supernatural powers she can use. If only she can find the key to the cloak, her mother will take care of her again.

Our faith in mother's magic dies slowly. Maybe it never disappears completely. Every time we play the lottery, sigh with pleasure at *Pretty Woman,* or sing "Do You Believe in Magic," we return to those happy days when wishing made it so.

Certainly the queen doesn't want to give up. She tries and tries to get the cloak to work for her, but mother's magic is not transferable. Mother's power remains undimmed in the queen's memory, but the queen can't seem to gain control of it for herself.

If we could only go through life as a child. If only someone else would take care of us. No matter how old I get, or how successfully I negotiate the real world, a little piece of my heart remains in childhood. That's the part that makes me laugh at pig races and lets me find enchantment at the circus.

But it can be a treacherous piece, letting me think life is simple and that someone will take care of me forever. Popular culture says that person will be my husband, and popular religion encourages me to believe that if I accept God like a child, miracles happen. I will live happily ever after. If only it were true.

This hope is what traps the queen, and after watching the colors and pattern fade time after time, it finally defeats her. Or so it seems. In truth, unless the queen abandons her efforts to extract magic from her mother's cloak, she'll never know her own powers. This episode focuses on a small defeat which will be forgotten by and by; but to the queen, her sense of loss is no less for that right now.

I V

Have you sought the help of the wise
woman?" asked the maid.
"No," said the Queen. "I didn't know
there was one in the kingdom.
"Oh, yes. She lives in a little house at
the edge of the wood."

Barbara Boggs Sigmund was the mayor of Princeton, New Jersey. When she died of cancer in the summer of 1990, there was a tremendous outpouring of grief. Not only did her friends mourn her passing, but people who barely knew her joined in celebrating her life because she had made such a difference in their world.

My friend Regina Podhorin, the director of Womanspace, Inc., was one of the people whose lives had been changed. Barbara had been her mentor. After she died, Regina tried to describe what that relationship meant to her.

> I knew all along that I was one of many who looked to Barbara Boggs Sigmund for guidance and support. Although she knew I watched her every move, she never made me feel like an observer. She always made me feel very special by including me as a peer.
>
> Even though we never discussed it, she had a way of sending me subtle messages showing approval, support, occasionally even displeasure. It was as if we had a special language that no one else could understand.
>
> Barbara never accepted failure from anyone. If I expressed frustration or uncertainty, she refused it

without judgment. The unspoken, but clear, message was—try again, you can do it.

If I could put into one sentence what Barbara did for me, it would be that she always trusted me and had confidence in me, more than I had in myself.

The hardest part of losing a mentor like this is knowing that I will never be able to replace her. I treasure the short time I had with her. I'm frightened to be alone, but now I must believe in myself the way she believed in me.

Fortunately, I can still hear her voice and see her face. It's a piece of me forever. In many ways, I guess it *is* me.

Although mentors like this woman are rare, wise women can come in many guises. For example, a friend of mine would never have become a clergywoman without the stabilizing influence of her own woman pastor, who was the only positive female role model in her life. Women therapists, especially those who work to empower you, are also wise women.

One thing they all have in common is their determination not to fashion a self for someone else; they won't even try. Perhaps that is why I have always put my grandmother in this category. She came from Maine, and she was a rock for me. She lived a few blocks away and the older I got the more time I spent with her. Despite the great difference in our ages, she eventually became my confidant.

Grandmother was a woman of firm principles, not all of which I shared. For example, she was a life member of the Women's Christian Temperance Union, and she also never approved of smoking. But when I came over, she would pick up a large conch shell and hand it to me. "For your cigarettes," she would say.

After she died, my aunt asked me if there was anything of Grandma's I would like. Without hesitation I asked for the conch shell, and to this day it sits in my living room as a memorial to her. Although many years have passed, I think of her still—the way she put people before principles and how, throughout her ninety-five years, she was always willing to learn and grow.

If you are lucky, you already know someone like Barbara Sigmund, my grandmother, the woman pastor, or a therapist who can encourage and support you. Whether or not you do, you can always find a wise woman in your own psyche.

Just like the ladies-in-waiting, the wise woman in "The Queen's Cloak" is a member of a woman's own internal cast of characters. For years, psychoanalysts have recognized the archetypal wise man, who often appears in men's dreams or stories as a wizard or an ancient gnome, like Yoda in *Star Wars*. Women need a similar figure to teach and advise them, but examples in myth and fiction are harder to find. No wonder the queen was unaware there was a wise woman in the kingdom!

That is ridiculous," said the Queen, stamping her foot. "I can't possibly do all those things myself. Besides, I don't need a magic cloak. I am the Queen."

For those of us brought up on princess tales, the instructions of the wise woman come as a shock. During these winter months, the queen has already struggled with her passivity and with her childlike longing that mother will still provide. Now comes another jolt.

There is no fairy godmother in "The Queen's Cloak." No one is going to wave a magic wand and present the queen with a new wardrobe. She must make her own cloak. Furthermore, even before she begins to weave, she will have to accomplish a variety of tasks that seem impossible to complete.

It is no wonder the queen had a fit. Never having met a wise woman, she had no way of knowing what one was like. A fairy godmother does good things for you. She comes to your house. Obviously, a wise woman does neither. You go to her, and you do all the work.

Who needs her? The queen. The queen needs the wise woman very much. She needs someone who will give her a workable recipe or directions and then expect her to follow through for herself. A fairy godmother, for all her charm, reinforces our passivity. Only a wise woman empowers us.

Unfortunately, many of us have come to expect a magic wand. Contemporary society teaches us that someone or something else will intervene to solve our problems. This message is repeated on so many levels, and in so many ways, that we can eventually doubt our ability to work things out ourselves. Certainly, the queen has no faith in her own abilities.

Believing she is inept, the queen takes refuge in her social role. In a culture that identifies people by their work, this response seems natural. We pigeonhole others according to their function. We are wife, mother, teacher, lawyer, divorced person, older woman, widow—not ourselves.

When my children were young, I was identified as "Marc and Danny's mother." When I go to Princeton Theological Seminary or Drew University, I am Dr. Engelsman. When I go to business affairs with my husband, I'm referred to as "Ralph's wife."

Everyone knows these roles are often comforting. They help other people relate to us and, when dealing with strangers, they give us some direction and a basis from which to act. They can even be a refuge.

On the other hand, most roles have little to do with our real nature. This means they restrict our growth. They can become straitjackets or Procrustean beds into which we try to fit. Sometimes we can adjust ourselves for awhile, but eventually we pay the price, if only in terms of resentment and irritation.

The worst part about social roles is their fragility. There is an ugly but true expression that describes how many of us live our lives—"only one man away from welfare." How precarious our status is when we must depend on our husbands for our total financial well-being.

A similar situation exists when we rely on others to furnish our sense of self. My divorced friends speak about their sense of loss and social confusion when they are no longer Mrs. So-and-so.

When the queen storms out of the wise woman's cottage, she has decided not to make the cloak. It is too hard; she has no confidence in her abilities. Now she retreats to the role she knows best. This won't be the last time she runs away, but who among us cannot sense the queen's growing panic and feel compassion for her? I imagine she is beginning to wish she had never found her mother's cloak.

*On the third day, she saw a face in the
mirror. It was sad and frightened. With a
shock, the Queen knew it was her own, and
she began to cry for herself. After weeping a
long time, the Queen stood up and called her
maid.*
"I have decided to make my own cloak."

When I first began to think about my self, who I might "really"
be, I always imagined that self in very positive terms. It was an
ideal. At the least, that self would have it "all together," be loving, serene, patient, and generally have all those qualities like
courage and strength which I often feel I lack. In other words,
my "self" would be perfect.

The queen felt the same way. As the years went by, perhaps she also fantasized about who she really was and what
she might do with her life, if she ever got the time. If this is true,
seeing her face in the mirror that dreadful day came as a terrible
shock; for without a doubt, she knew she had seen her true self,
yet that self was anything but pretty.

Despite all our protestations of humility, most of us think
that, all things being equal, we are really rather wonderful. Our
faults are temporary, and when we do or feel something bad,
we "don't know what came over us."

When the queen sees her sad and frightened face and
knows it is her self, she takes a tremendous step. She makes
contact with her own real being. It would be wonderful if we
could do this at a happy moment, and there is no reason why
we can't. But most of us don't. Many of us must be under du-
ress before we can see what is really there.

Meeting her self this way, the queen finds a person she
never expected. Behind the facade of boredom and depression

is fear and sorrow. The shock is thus twofold. Her self is not flawless. Furthermore, she has strong feelings she has kept buried. Despite the unexpected nature of this discovery, the queen has little choice but to accept what she finds.

Once the queen passes through this moment, she is well and truly launched on her quest. Certainly, her first response is to mourn her losses. By the time we are mature, most of us have many things to grieve—our youth, our past opportunities, our selves. These are among the real losses that come from our earlier choices.

I have a student who finds it almost impossible to make a decision. She talks about sitting on the fence looking over the fields on either side. She frequently says how hard it is to choose because every choice involves a loss.

Few of us can reach mid-life without having made some of these painful selections. Some of them have even been made at our own expense, because often it seems easier to give up ourselves than to risk the loss of an old relationship or the safety of an old role.

Part of our reluctance to choose is also fear. We fear the future, we fear changing. What lies ahead might actually be worse than what we already have, and we don't want risk, we want guarantees.

Although this may have been our lifelong pattern, when we mature the pendulum sometimes swings in a different direction. Now we are confronted with the reality of death. I was in my early thirties when a neighbor died of breast cancer. Many of us on the street were about her age, and all of us felt her death keenly. It was the first time I ever truly faced the possibility of dying. While visiting at that funeral home, all my youthful feelings of invulnerability simply evaporated.

Once the queen reaches mid-life, she may also find that her priorities have begun to shift. Knowing death will bring an end to all her possibilities certainly raises the ante. If the queen does not act for herself now, she may never have the chance. Decisions postponed, opportunities rejected, yearnings unsatisfied have begun to pile up. Eventually this mass of unlived life may tip the balance in favor of risk.

Perhaps this is what happens to the queen. She weeps; she mourns. But she also makes a decision for her self. Under the most adverse circumstances, she reaches out, in hope, for something new.

This great act of courage breaks an old pattern. Before this moment, the queen lived a fairly passive, dependent life—perhaps not on the surface but in relation to her own self. When she tells her maid she is going to make her own cloak, the queen visibly changes direction.

Sometimes we are able to look back and point out significant events or decisions which altered our lives. A few of these are obvious at the time—like who we decide to marry or even not to marry at all. Others are much more subtle; only much later can we look back and recognize their importance.

When I went to work at Womanspace, Inc., I was just helping out a friend. She was moving away and needed someone to run a few workshops. Seven years later, my relationship with that agency has become a major professional commitment. Now it is easy to see how a hastily arranged lunch changed my life. At the time, it seemed like nothing at all.

The queen's decision to make her cloak appears to be a conscious milestone. It feels like a beginning, the start of something new and challenging. But because the queen's search for her centered self actually began with the inventory of the castle, this decisive step does not mark the dawn of anything. In reality, this first meeting with her self, and her commitment to the cloak, comes after she has completed one quarter of her quest.

This is the way it is with winter. Things have been going on under the surface which will not be seen until the beginning of spring. A lot has already happened, and certainly the queen has done much more than she realizes.

SPRING

I

Since spring was just beginning, the Queen
decided to start by planting flax.

Of all the episodes in "The Queen's Cloak," there is none I return to more often than this one. It is probably the most boring, tedious, repetitive task facing the queen, but for many reasons it has come to hold pride of place in my life.

If someone wanted my biography, or was willing to listen to the ups and downs of my existence, they would never hear a word about planting flax. Nevertheless, it is crucial because planting flax is real, ordinary life. Day in and day out kind of life. Doing the best you can when you don't see much progress, or when the goal is so far off that the little bit you do today doesn't seem very important.

Most books I've read about spiritual or psychological development seem to be quite goal-oriented. The end is what matters. Whether it is union with the divine, enlightenment, or self-actualization, attention is focused on the goal and we only hear about the major stops along the way.

This concentration on the high points presents a very distorted picture. Years of hard, necessary, but unspectacular work are wiped away with a few lines of prose. A chapter ends, and the next begins with the words, "Several years later. . . ."

Planting flax is what goes on between the chapters. This is the work that represents what a student of mine appropriately described as the "laborious, unglamorous, and often menial" work that goes into becoming aware of your self. I think it also illustrates those long spells of aridity which dog any spiritual or psychological journey.

Omitting or glossing over this aspect of our effort has at least one terrible side effect. It can deceive us into believing that just because we know something in our head, we can do it. Authors of self-help books often are the worst offenders. Like the Pharisees of the Bible, they would make us twice the children of hell we were before we read their work. They tell us we should love more wisely, be more assertive, or express our feelings, but even when we agree with these goals, most of us still cannot change. Certainly, books like this always make me feel doubly stupid.

This gap between knowing in the head and knowing in the gut appears at many levels. A friend of mine once wrote to me wondering, "how many people go through therapy like I did, thinking if I could *just* figure this out . . . if I *just* had the insight." How many times have I said to someone, "I know, *I know*— but I still can't do it."

My husband calls this my "Billy Jean King syndrome." I play tennis and I've seen Billy Jean play. Not surprisingly, our games don't have much in common. But on the court, I've been known to berate myself when I don't do as well as she does. What I set aside in those moments of irritation are the thousands of practice hours Billy Jean has spent perfecting her skill. What I want instead is a visit from the fairy godmother of tennis.

Perhaps this is why I keep coming back to this episode. In matters of the psyche, as in tennis, there are no quick transformations. We pay for them by doing hard, dull, repetitive work. We plant flax. Each time we do this, we remind ourselves that our development is a process, and we won't see the results right away. If this delay is as frustrating to you as it can be to me, this kind of spiritual gardening can teach us to be patient with ourselves.

Planting flax also reminds me of the physical dimension of the self, which many of us were brought up to deny, minimize, or ignore. Even today, young girls are getting mixed messages. The other day, I went into a children's store and saw a little girl in a frilly jumpsuit. She was making a halfhearted effort to play with some little boys, but her clothes kept getting in the way. Finally, her mother told her to sit in the rocking chair. It was depressing to see that some girls are still being taught to put appearance and dress before themselves.

Women raised before Jane Fonda were taught that sweating was not ladylike. Now we know physical activity helps *everyone* stay healthy, and walking, running, or swimming replenishes our energy. As we reach mid-life, exercise also enables us to live better. It improves our ability to manage the strong emotions which can beset us as they do the queen. Because it can help us blow off steam in a healthy way, those who are not getting much exercise might want to reevaluate this aspect of their lives.

Thus, the rewards of planting flax are several. It helps anchor the psyche in the real world and teaches the queen the organic nature of real change. The joy of this labor is that she can rely on its results. Whenever the going gets rough, the queen returns to her field. She looks at the plants and draws satisfaction and encouragement from what she has already done.

This is not like a pat on the back from a false friend who says "I always knew you could do it." Looking at the field, the queen remembers her aches and pains; she also remembers how she set aside her habitual passivity to work actively on her own behalf. The strength the queen derives from this awareness is that of tensile steel, which no one can take away from her.

*But on the day it was finished, the Queen
laughed. Running to her horse, she brought
out a picnic she had hidden in her saddle. Like
a pair of conspirators, she and her maid
celebrated together.*

This moment of celebration seems to be the right place to examine the relationship between the queen and her maid. When I
do workshops on "The Queen's Cloak," one of the first comments is usually "I wish I had a maid." The remark is almost
always accompanied by a sigh.

Who is this woman, anyway? One of my students was
sufficiently upset by the maid's role in the story that she soundly
rebuked me for writing such an elitist tale. Unfortunately, she
missed the point. The maid is not like the wise woman, who
many of us know or have known in real life. This character represents an aspect of women's psyches that is rarely personified.
I believe she is a personification of our egos, that ill–treated,
underappreciated, and much maligned aspect of our selves.

From the time we are small, most of us are taught to
keep our egos in their place, which is clearly subordinate. Because society especially encourages women to serve others, to
put others' needs before their own, one of the greatest put–
downs is to call a woman "selfish," "self-centered," or "egotis-
tical." Our culture tells us over and over that caring for others is
the best way to fulfill ourselves. Even popular religion constantly
exhorts us to put service before self.

If you are getting uncomfortable, let me say a few words
on behalf of our egos before you banish them to the servants'
hall. The ethics of most Western religions have been designed
for and by ruling-class males. That is why various books of the
Bible contain instructions on the treatment of slaves, servants,

widows, and orphans. Virtue, for the owners or male relatives of such people, consists of caring for their needs. Virtue for members of the underclass is to be obedient.

Although this description is grossly oversimplified, it does illustrate how responsible behavior varies depending on one's position. Because I believe this is still true, I think it is important to note what might be appropriate behavioral differences today. For successful men, who get their egos stroked by many people in many ways, an admonition to put others first is necessary. For a generation who can't wait to get the best of everything, it is vital.

But for women (and men) in subordinate positions with few sources of support—and this is actually most of us—this message can be a sentence of death. Many women writers have spoken truthfully about this reality. So do battered women. Always putting others before yourself, feeling guilty about doing something for yourself if it causes someone else any inconvenience, leads to more than low self-esteem. It can be life threatening.

Even in the most ordinary matters, women are still taught to put others first. For example, during the years when my children were young, my friends and I realized that we were either well and able to cope, or in the hospital. As mothers and wives, we were not allowed to be just plain sick.

Many years ago I came down with the twenty-four-hour flu—the kind we used to call the "Green Death." My husband got me home from a meeting, and when I staggered into bed I felt so awful, I wished I *had* died. About half an hour later, he reappeared in the doorway. "Honey," he said in an apologetic voice, "Marc just threw up in his room. I guess he has the same thing. But if I try to clean it up, you know I'll get sick, too. Won't you do it?" Guess who crawled down the hall and took care of our son?

If the message to put service before self prevails even in such minor matters as these, it indicates how subversive this attitude really is. Later in the spring, the queen will begin to grapple with some of the ramifications of this education; but before that can happen, she must make friends with her ego.

In "The Queen's Cloak," the maid is the queen's best friend. Without her assistance, there would be no cloak. She is the one who remembers the note; she knows where to find a wise woman. The maid arranges to have the field plowed and helps the queen plant the flax. Later, when the queen leaves to visit her sister, the maid rescues the enterprise one more time by tucking the piece of cloak among the many packages on the mule.

As a representation of the queen's ego, she promotes the active, practical, supportive side of her psyche. Unlike our superegos, which can be tyrannical slave drivers full of expressions like "you should do this," "you must do that," and "never do the other," most women's egos are quiet friends that have our best interest at heart.

I think the reason so many women wish they had a maid is the same reason most women I know wish they had a wife. We all yearn for someone to take care of us—at least from time to time. We all wish for someone who would do for us what we find ourselves doing for others.

Last year, one of our sons, his wife, and their three-month-old child moved in with us for five months. Never before had a woman been in my house who wasn't a guest. Not since my two sons had moved out had anyone stayed so long. Because we recognized the changes this visit would make in all our lives, we tried to avert as many potential problems as possible. I think we managed quite well.

The one thing I hadn't planned on was the joy. Not only the joy of being with my grandson, but the sheer joy of having another woman in the house! We alternated cooking dinner and cleaning up. If she was awake half the night with a teething baby, I would watch my grandson while she napped. If I had to finish a report, she would do whatever had to be done, remembering all the details, while I kept at it.

When they left, I was glad to get my house back and they were equally happy to be home. But I missed them. Most of all, I missed someone who understood caring as only another woman could.

The irony in all this is clear. I am a woman who could care for myself—but I rarely do. Neither do most women I know. One woman said, "caring for yourself is too much work." Although I don't know all the reasons for her comment, many women share this view. We were discussing how hard it is to get some men to share equally in the housework. Even if you have an agreement, they tend to slack off—not out of malice but because our culture says it is not their job. And if you insist, many have their way of getting even. "'Honey . . . do you put bleach in the white wash?' he says, interrupting my work. By the time he finishes playing helpless, it would have been easier to do it myself."

But there are many levels of caring beyond the obvious. For example, my husband helps: he roots for me, and he also listens carefully, thus helping me find my own solutions. But he rarely does the little things that constitute so much of women's caring, nor does he understand why, if it's important, it is so hard for me to do those things for myself.

These are some of the reasons why I often think about this episode of the fairy tale. Here the queen selects a minor character in the story to be her ally and life companion. The maid differs from the ladies-in-waiting: she is active, they are passive. She is resourceful, they are not. Judging her by what she does, the ego-maid is always a reliable and faithful friend of the queen's centered self. When the queen recognizes and celebrates their relationship, she helps prepare herself for the trials yet to come.

In real life, of course, there are often similarities between those who function in our lives like the maid and the wise woman. An analyst I know immediately identified with the maid. In her practice, she said, "I assist the process of another." She is a faithful, practical friend to the self, standing beside it throughout the therapy. This capacity to facilitate our growth becomes the hallmark of the best helpers in our lives.

III

Now I have to take back something I gave my husband and each of my children. The Queen knew they would be angry, because no one likes to give up something they think is theirs.

This is one of the episodes in "The Queen's Cloak" where the connection between our inner and outer life is very clear. In order for the queen to continue following the instructions of the wise woman, she must change her relationships to those closest to her. She must take back several things she gave her husband and children, and she cannot tell them why.

Among the various qualities we need to reclaim are those our culture does not encourage women to possess. Because human nature is similar, regardless of sex, women have the same yearnings as men. We want power and respect; we are ambitious; we want to be cared for. Yet by characterizing these feelings as wrong or aberrant, and teaching women to deny them, society's standards inhibit women's development.

One way to handle disapproved interests is to project them onto those nearest and dearest. This time-honored strategy at least gives us a chance to enjoy these qualities, if only vicariously. This method of dealing with aptitudes, aspirations, and feelings that society does not support in women has been around so long, and is so ingrained, that it seems almost natural.

Most woman who read "The Queen's Cloak" immediately understand the challenge facing the queen. We all know we have projected bits of ourselves onto family members and friends. Some of these pieces are quite big, and many are obvious. These are among the ones the queen must recover and use for her own cloak. But as I continue to reflect on this episode, I keep finding additional parts of myself scattered around the landscape. Obviously, each woman projects different parts of herself; therefore, there is no generic list. What we share is the habit of pushing off those parts of ourselves we do not like.

Although we understand the purpose of reclaiming our own stuff from others, doing so is something else. Social customs and values not only cap our self-expression, they encourage men and children to think they are entitled to our energy, talents, and affection. If and when we say no, all hell can break loose.

Women who want to make their own cloak, to be centered in themselves, run very real risks, and the price of wholeness can be high. Because "The Queen's Cloak" is a fairy tale, a long metaphor about the process of becoming whole, the queen manages to take back what she needs from her family without causing any serious disruption in her relationships. Those who recognize the importance of what the queen does and try to do it in their own lives may not be so lucky. The wise woman warned that making one's own cloak can be difficult and dangerous work. Taking back what is projected onto others is this kind of struggle.

For women brought up in families and in an era where everything they did, from dinner parties to dissertations, was supposed to seem effortless, this passage can be especially hard. I remember my mother-in-law giving me a cookbook entitled *Never in the Kitchen When Company Comes*. According to the author, all the work could be done in advance, thus allowing the hostess to be with her guests and look cool. "Never let them see you sweat" is an admonition with a long history.

In order to minimize the effort we actually make, we were also taught to say, "It was nothing." Recently, my husband and I went to an old-fashioned holiday party. Everything was outstanding, but when I praised our hostess for her wonderful dinner, she brushed off my compliments. This commonplace example saddens me because it reminds me, once again, of the way women have been taught to make light of their work.

Taking back what we have projected onto others should never be glossed over. The effort and pain which go into making one's own cloak is never more evident than in the following sections. In her book on life after menopause, Christine Downing remarks that "we all really know: there are initiations beyond those associated with adolescence that are difficult and lonely" (Downing 1987, p. 7). Because we are reimaging and renegotiating our relationships with those near and dear, working through this part is hard, lonely work.

From the beginning, the queen chafes under the wise woman's admonition to keep her reasons to herself. She thinks that by telling her family why she wants to take back her various gifts, the exchange will be a peaceful one. Unfortunately, even getting consent in advance rarely helps. When I went back to graduate school, I carefully explained to my husband and children how my studies would probably keep me from doing many things I had done in the past. For about six weeks they were quite understanding, then they got angry. In retrospect, it seems to me they complained about every single alteration in their life-style they could possibly lay at my door. If there was an easy way past this sticky wicket, I didn't know it. In the end, it took more than a year to renegotiate the way we lived together. Because they couldn't calculate the cost to themselves in advance, getting their approval before I enrolled was meaningless. Eventually, I had to take responsibility for my own actions regardless of their reactions.

One of the greatest stumbling blocks to this effort is what I call the Male Entitlement Syndrome. If men want something you have, they feel entitled to take it, use it, spend it, borrow it, or, as Ntozake Shange says, run off with it (Shange 1975, p. 52–54). Ironically, the acronym (MES) is what it causes in women's lives!

Several months ago, I stepped out of the shower and reached for my deodorant. It wasn't there. After a quick search, I realized my now quite liberated husband had probably taken it with him to California. He didn't ask, he didn't even tell me.

He just took it. Later that same morning, while waiting for a student, I was talking with a friend about how many men act the same way. We were comparing notes, joking in a not-so-funny way about the secret school all men must attend to learn about their right to our stuff, when my student arrived—thirty minutes late. When I told her what we were discussing, she got a strange look on her face. "You may not believe this," she said, "but the reason I'm late is because my husband took my car. His is in the shop. He didn't say anything to me, he just assumed I had no plans. I had to call him at his office and get him to bring it back. I'm sorry I'm late."

These relatively minor examples refer to possessions. The more subtle and dangerous forms of male entitlement have to do with our love, support, energy, understanding, and care. The most horrific cases involve battered women who are cut off from family, friends, employers, the world. Their abusers exercise absolute control and power over the women in their lives; they want sole rights to everything they have to give. Nothing can be denied them or held back for another.

Between these ghastly examples and the merely annoying lies an undertow of male neediness which we have to struggle against in order to claim any energy for ourselves. Some men flatter us, some weep, some threaten to leave us. Others will sabotage our efforts or show outright hostility. There are as many strategies and methods employed as there are degrees of need.

Most of the time, we are flattered. We like to feel needed. After all, society tells us this is the way to womanly fulfillment. No wonder the queen must make friends with her ego before she tackles this part of her labors. Unless she believes she has a right to be happy, to be a centered self, to use her energy and talents for herself as well as for others, she will never find the fortitude to withdraw unneeded support from her husband and children.

*"Good husband, do you remember your
coronation robe which I embroidered with
gold thread?"*

The first challenge facing the queen is to retrieve those qualities she has projected onto her husband. In our culture, some of the most common attributes are the capacity to operate in the real world (particularly in matters of business and finance) and the ability to exercise power.

Power and agency are often associated with older men. Although this fairy tale focuses on the queen's husband, in real life these qualities are frequently projected onto one's father, older brother, clergyman, professor, or charismatic politician. The problems which appear in many of these other relationships are similar to those between king and queen. Because we often scatter our projections this way, you will eventually want to explore your associations with many men.

When the queen embroidered her husband's coronation robe, she transferred her own capacity for personal power and authority to him. She let him make the major decisions and gave him the last word on everything. A woman in one of my workshops even described the golden thread as "the golden praise women shower on their husbands to build them up."

Because men are accustomed to this preeminence, the queen's plan to repossess his royal robe makes him feel diminished and afraid: "No one will know I'm a king," he says. Once these words could have frightened or manipulated the queen, but now her ego is stronger, and she has the courage to point out the fallacy of his reasoning.

He has always had his own power and authority. Bearing the projected qualities of the queen may have made him feel more important, but the burden has a negative effect as well. It undercuts his own self-awareness and feeds a sense of neediness the king wants to surmount. Thus, when the queen reclaims her own capacities, he is able to exercise his own attributes more freely than before.

Because it is always a struggle to regain these projected abilities, in real life this act of reclamation takes a long time. One clergywoman I know repeats the phrase "take ye the authority" whenever she feels overwhelmed by feelings of weakness and indecision. This paraphrase of the bishop's words at her ordination has become a mantra of sorts which she chants to remind herself of who she is and what she can really do. Perhaps we each need a phrase like that to help us focus on the task at hand.

Next the Queen went to her son. Hanging on the wall was a small tapestry on which she had woven her family's coat of arms.

One of the most likely qualities for the queen to project onto a son (or, sometimes, onto a talented daughter, young coworker, or student) is ambition. This is another characteristic most of us are taught to deny in ourselves.

When the queen made him the tapestry containing her coat-of-arms, she projected her personal hopes onto her son. Encouraging him to fulfill her dreams would enable her to live through him. When she reclaims the wall hanging, he is resentful and confused. Having tried to adopt her agenda as his own, he feels cut adrift when it is taken away.

Now it is up to the queen to explain that he could never have taken possession of *her* kingdom or achieved *her* goals. Once she relieves him of this burden, the son realizes he has dreams of his own, which he is now free to explore.

Reclaiming our ambitions is also a slow process. Once we repossess them, we alone become responsible for working them out. Many will prove to be unrealistic, others may have to be abandoned for lack of money, time, ability, or support. Although this time of appraisal is usually a period of painful reassessment, the hopes that remain or the dreams that can be adapted are truly our own. These realistic ambitions are the ones we can fulfill.

Finally, she went to see her daughter. "My dear," she said nervously, "do you remember the afghan I made you when you were little?"

Reclaiming something from our daughters (nieces, goddaughters, or other young women in our lives) represents a slightly different problem. Projection is still the issue, but because of the close mother–daughter bond, it may be even harder to break.

What the queen must take back is the *excess* of caring. Most of us have been taught to look after everyone but ourselves and to deny ourselves the tender, loving care we also need. Under these unrealistic conditions, many of us take the little girl within ourselves and project her onto our daughters. Only once she is projected outside ourselves can we coddle and protect her.

This rather convoluted situation often leads to an overidentification of mother and daughter. Only if we recognize our own needs and resolve to take care of ourselves can many of us stop overnurturing our daughters.

Reappropriating the child within, and loving her, thus becomes one of the major tasks facing the queen. The problem is symbolized by an afghan the daughter still uses, one she plans to hand on to her own child. How can the queen reclaim that yarn for herself and still show her daughter the depth of her love?

The answer comes from the queen's increasing awareness. Perhaps she can help her daughter learn how to care for herself. A most touching moment occurred at the end of one of my workshops when a mother and daughter took me aside. With pride shining from her eyes, the young woman told me how her mother had taught her to make her own cloak.

When we give our daughters the opportunity to make something of their own, we help them realize they are neither our clones nor helpless children. The queen's daughter needs a bigger afghan and prefers different colors and patterns. By teaching her how to make a new one, we give her the gift of our knowledge and set her free to fulfill her self.

Although these tasks are difficult and painful, withdrawing projections ultimately helps everyone. As one of my students commented, when the queen shows each member of her family "how they can stand apart from her and grow, she gives herself the same freedom." This is a precious gift the queen must give herself and others. But it is not easy, and reclaiming our projected pieces takes a long time.

—————— IV ——————

*After the Queen had collected something she
had made from every member of her family,
she took out her mother's cloak. Carefully she
cut it in half from neck to hem. She quickly
took apart one half and set it aside for her
own cape. After deftly catching the threads
along the edge of the other piece, she wrapped
it so it could be sent to her sister.*

*"Half and half. I think that's fair, don't
you?" said the Queen, making a face.*

After the stress of repossessing various items from members of her family, the queen is probably quite relieved to return to her apartments. There she can finally catch her breath and occupy herself with the apparently mundane task of dividing her mother's cloak.

But this simple act opens a whole new dimension to her quest. During the winter months, the queen struggles to give up the magical mother—the one she remembers from childhood who took care of her and could read her mind. But after the wise woman says that even she cannot unlock the mystery of her mother's cloak, the queen probably thinks she is through with it.

Nothing could be further from the truth. Once the queen has abandoned her infantile images of mother, she must begin to deal with her parent as a real woman. Her first response to this challenge is to divide mother in half.

Although this episode is very brief, and easy to overlook, it is extremely important. When the queen turns back to her mother, she separates the cloak. Her intention is to keep the good memories and attributes of her mother for herself; she will send her sister, who is already hated and ignored, everything associated with the "bad" mother. Indeed, what could be fairer than that!

Of course, the real problem lies in the division, not which half of mother's split image we want to retain. In our culture, we have been taught to think and believe dualistically, so it is extremely easy to slip into this frame of mind. Our society and religion promote it. We have light/dark, male/female, mind/body, good girls/bad girls, god and the devil. Even though we know better, my old professor Will Herberg was right. "The culture works on us in our sleep." Under the circumstances, nothing seems more natural than to compartmentalize our memories and our friends.

If this is the prevailing ethos, why should we bother to challenge it? I believe we have to challenge it because it is deceptive and certainly wrong as a stratagem for anyone who wants a centered self.

Those of us raised in cultures dominated by Western philosophy have to go outside our tradition to find more holistic images of life and the divine. Whenever we find them in mandalas, in Eastern religions, or in the cultures of non–Western people, many of us respond with joy. But integrating these visions into our dualistic consciousness presents more problems than one might suppose. Even at the end of her labors, the queen must still struggle to visualize herself as a whole.

As I return to this episode over and over, I continue to marvel at the tenacity of the dualistic image and the grip it has on my life. One way to confront this problem is to explore rigorously the splits in one's own psyche. Fortunately, when the queen divides her mother's cloak in half, she actually sets in motion a chain of events which will help her do just that.

Like most of us, the queen chooses the good image of her mother. The memories she wants to hold close are the happy ones: those of comfort and support, of shared confidences, of trust which is virtually unmatchable. We can add to that list the exploration of new things, working together, bedtime stories, laughter shared, tears dried, illness healed, special meals and foods. We all have our own sacred catalog of remembrances which we share, especially at holidays and other special occasions.

Thinking of these things makes me want to stop writing and bake some chocolate chip cookies. My mother was not particularly fond of cooking, nor was she a baker. But every now and then, usually on a cold, rainy Saturday afternoon, she would suggest that we make cookies together.

In the days before mixes and mixers, we started from scratch, and we stirred the heavy dough with a spoon. A more adept cook would have had a supply of wooden spoons in her kitchen, but Mom used the serving spoons from an ornate set of silver plate she never liked. Eventually they became dented and a little bent, but they worked perfectly well—except for chocolate chip cookies.

Whether I stirred too vigorously or the dough was too heavy for the spoon, occasionally it would snap. The first time it happened, I was shocked, standing there with the fancy stem in my hand and a stricken look on my face. My mother just laughed. Then she dug out the bowl of the spoon, and using her finger she popped some of the delicious raw dough in my mouth. She did the same for herself. After we cleaned the broken spoon this way, she gave me another and we finished the job.

About ten years ago, my parents moved to a retirement community. Their small apartment would only accommodate a fraction of their belongings, so Mom sent me many things, including most of her silver. As I unwrapped the felt cases, I discovered all the ornate silver plate she disliked—complete with three broken serving spoons. I suppose I should have them fixed, but I know I never will. They bring back too many happy memories the way they are.

These are the kind of treasures the queen keeps for herself. Let her sister have the dross, she will keep the best. Isn't that what her mother said—take what you want and send the rest to your sister? We know the queen is unfortunately mistaken. But for now, she thinks she has finished her work. Certainly she is oblivious to the way she has distorted her mother's message and to the trace of anger which flares when she mentions her sister.

*From my sister? Nothing," said the Queen
angrily. "She is a terrible person. I have
neither seen nor spoken to her since before I
was married. I have not made her anything."
    "Not even when you were young?"
    The Queen started to answer as before
when suddenly she remembered. "Oh, no!
When I was fourteen, I made her a shawl to
look like the starry heavens. I can't ask her for
that. She would kill me."*

One evening, while traveling in France, I sat outside writing a letter to my parents. The weather had been perfect, but as I looked at the darkening sky, I saw a little cloud no bigger than my hand. The next day it rained; it actually rained steadily for the next three weeks. All the rivers flooded; they even closed the Rhine to river traffic. Who would have expected such a small token could foretell such a large storm?

Certainly the queen never suspects her small snit would be very significant. But when the wise woman mentions the sister, the storm brewing in the queen's heart breaks with full force. The wise woman is stupid, the task is too hard, and she gallops home in a fury. Obviously, being a wise woman isn't always a popular job.

Once the queen's temper cools, she finds herself confronted by more unpleasant feelings. First rage and then fear flash across her interior landscape. Who would not be terrified by so much passion? Certainly those of us brought up to be "proper ladies" can be quite shaken.

Who is this sister and why does she have such power to upset us? She may be a real person. One of my friends scribbled the following comment in the margin of this manuscript. "I have a friend, 35, who hasn't spoken to her sister for at least five years! At holidays they sit at table and say to their mother, 'Please ask Mary to pass the butter.' And they are *intelligent* women!"

As we have learned, intelligence has little to do with it. Indeed, sometimes sisters do grievous things to one another, and that pain must not be minimized. Family fights can be horrific, in part because family members know where and how to hurt each other the most. If you are caught in this situation, you may want to consider seeking a rapprochement or some resolution with your sister which will allow you to reclaim at least part of the energy you now spend disliking her.

But whether or not you have a real sister with whom you are on good terms or bad, all of us have a psychic sister who has been the garbage dump for all our negative projections. Carl Jung calls her our shadow, and Esther Harding warns us that mid-life may require a greater coming to terms with her than we thought possible when we were young (Jung 1951, pp. 8–10; Harding 1975, p. 243).

In the main, this psychic sister carries all those traits and tendencies which belong to us but which we find unacceptable and want to deny. Some of these are culturally conditioned. For example, those of us brought up to be "ladies" or to emulate them are supposed to be well-mannered, soft-spoken, even-tempered, fair-minded, trusting, and monogamous. Given these restraints, what happens to those feelings, ideas, opinions, and behaviors that do not fit the model?

Enter our psychic sister. Like an imaginary playmate who does all our bad deeds, she is the one we blame. Unfortunately, this fantasy figure rarely goes unrealized. Most of the time, we know someone with one or two characteristics we don't like. Why not dump all our rejected stuff on them? What a convenience. This way we can hate them and deny even the existence of our negative self.

Everyone uses this strategy; the only differences are in degree. According to my own experience, and that of my students, the more aspects of our personality we deny, the stronger our shadow becomes. What we project onto our shadow slides increasingly outside our access and control until, eventually, these alienated pieces of our personality assume an independent existence which is at odds with our conscious personality. Thus, the more we reject our shadow self, the more frightening it often seems to be. Certainly the queen has become terrified of hers.

There is no way we can reclaim material from the shadow without confronting it. Each of us knows at least some of what lies buried in our own dark side. Greed, envy, sloth, and selfishness are a few obvious candidates for rejection. Religion and society condemn these qualities, and most of us cooperate by trying to stamp them out of ourselves.

As adult women, we also possess certain other attributes which our culture decrees are wrong especially when they appear in women, namely, anger and sexuality. Unfortunately, these supposedly negative characteristics are closely related to one's energy level; therefore, whenever we assign these attributes to our shadow we lose much of our zest and creativity. Finally, our negative self carries those traits—some petty, some serious—we personally find offensive.

All these aspects of the shadow are represented by the dark shawl the queen must recover from her sister. The prospect is frightening, but making her own cloak is now the most important thing. Thus, when the queen contemplates a visit to her sister, she takes the first step in reclaiming pieces of this hidden treasure. Now her dream of a centered self finally outweighs the habits of a lifetime.

As for me, no matter how much I want to avoid this episode in "The Queen's Cloak," I find myself returning to it over and over. When I realize it may be necessary to repossess some piece of my self I would just as soon ignore, I feel like the queen. Each time I scowl at the planted flax, I think this will be the last time I have to welcome some despised part of my self into my consciousness.

Perhaps it is the nature of our labors that we cannot do the work once and for all. In my experience, and in that of my students, we end up doing a little bit now, a little bit later. In dealing with our shadow, this means we will often denounce the wise woman who tells us to greet our sister and run away like the queen. Fortunately, it is possible to revisit the rows of flax and draw courage from our past work.

What a strange way to end the spring.

SUMMER

I

*Early one summer day, when all was ready,
the Queen left for her sister's kingdom. She
was dressed in beautiful clothes and rode a
white horse. Her trunks were filled with fine
clothes and jewelry and lovely presents. All
these were packed on a mule which followed
the royal horse.*

*In her excitement, the Queen forgot her
sister's piece of the cloak. But the maid
remembered, and she tucked the package
among the many boxes on the mule.*

What a elegant image! The queen looks like she stepped right
out of a fairy tale. I bet she was even wearing her crown. Everything is perfect, right down to the liveried soldiers who will
ride with her to the border. Banners are waving, and the people
cheer as she makes her way through the kingdom. What could
be wrong with this picture?

Several things are not quite right. Because they do not
appear to effect the outcome of the story, we may want to shrug
them off. Nevertheless, the underlying theme of this section
needs to be mentioned.

Bruce Springsteen has a song in which he sings about
taking "one step up and two steps back." His phrase reverses
the well-known words of encouragement many of us say to
ourselves when we struggle with difficult material. Springstein's
words visualize a very different scenario, one more appropriate for Sisyphus, who fruitlessly labors to push the rock up the
mountain.

His song captures the essence of this episode. Having
made the courageous decision to visit her sister, the queen now

loses ground. She falls back on her royal persona, the same one she has lived out of for years, the same one she threw in the face of the wise woman the first time they met. Now, like snow in July, the insights of winter and spring seem to vanish, leaving the queen very like she was at the beginning of the story.

Because it reflects the truth of psychological and spiritual experience, this particular episode actually comforts me. Once I set my mind to something, I want to move forward in a straight line. If progress must be slow, at least let it be steady. The queen's setback reminds me that my preference for continuous progress has little bearing on reality. Thus, when I find myself acting out of old patterns, even when I "know" better, I reflect on this part of "The Queen's Cloak."

Despite reverting to an earlier stage, the queen's mission is saved because her maid remembers the true purpose of the journey. It is not to impress her sister or appease her wrath. Her sole tasks are to deliver half of their mother's cloak and to get back the shawl she made to look like the starry heavens. These two pieces of cloth, then, set the mood for this summer journey.

Several of my students have commented on the lack of an evil element in "The Queen's Cloak." To be sure, there is no wicked witch or dragon. Unlike St. George or Dorothy in Oz, there aren't any monsters the queen must slay; therefore, at least superficially, this evaluation is true. But as we follow the queen through the next months, the darker aspects of the story become evident.

Not only is this a somber season for the queen, it is a lonely one. Because she journeys inward, she must travel unaccompanied. Once she crosses into her sister's kingdom, the queen loses not only her clothes but also her royal title. These are unnecessary items on such a personal mission.

When the queen embarks on this aspect of her labors, she is fearful and unsure of herself, so who would blame her for carrying all the accoutrements of her position? They make a pretty show, and they give her confidence, even though they soon will be irrelevant.

*Not long afterwards, a man appeared from
the woods. He barred the way with his sword
and ordered the Queen off her horse. Pushing
her to the side of the road, he pawed through
the rich gifts. When he saw the remnant from
her mother's cloak, he laughed.*

*"Give me your clothes. You can wrap
yourself in this old rag."*

*As soon as she was naked, he looked at
her and laughed again.*

*"You are a dried-up old stick, aren't
you."*

*Then the man gathered up all her
belongings, took her horse and mule, and
disappeared as quietly as he had come.*

Disaster has struck. No sooner is the queen on her own when
she is confronted by her "worst-case scenario." Surely, if there
is an evil figure in "The Queen's Cloak," it is the thief.

As I mentioned, many of the characters in the fairy tale
can represent real people, as well as parts of our psyche. The
thief is one of these dual figures, and it is important to examine
all the ways he affects our lives.

To begin with reality, we all know or have met the negative male. Virtually every woman who has attended my workshops or classes can relate to the terror experienced by the queen
when the thief steps out of the woods. We all fear the mugger
or rapist; many of us have experienced his brutality.

Even those of us who have not been set upon by a
stranger have probably had some frightening moments with
men we know. These are not occasions in my life I want to remember, so I tend not to think about them except in the ab-

stract. I don't want to recall near misses with date rape or being molested by a trusted teacher. One thing I do know is that these events are not unique to me, but something I share with millions of women.

As women in this culture, we are familiar with all kinds of degrading, violent, and abusive encounters which make us feel out of control. We have been victimized, and we have often been told it was our own fault. We were in the wrong place, wore the wrong clothes, sent the wrong signals, used poor judgment. This episode evokes our memories of such encounters.

Of course, not all of our experiences are physical. Many of them are mental or emotional attacks by men we love. In many ways, they hurt the most. Is there a woman alive who has not felt exploited or betrayed by some man? Even on a superficial level, what girl's heart has not been broken, if only by a callow youth who never knew we dreamt of loving him?

Recalling these events, whether they are mild or bitter, is one of the hardest tasks facing the queen. How I would like to say this work is unnecessary, but a woman who wants to make her own cloak needs to remember these sad, difficult, if not terrifying, events. The energy we have tied up in repressing them needs to be liberated.

Nevertheless, no matter how many times I have had to think on this episode of "The Queen's Cloak," I never return to it without repugnance. One of the reasons it is extremely difficult for me is because, like most of us, I was raised to expect men to save and protect me, to take care of me forever. If nothing else, this experience with the thief takes away such illusions.

There is no Prince Charming in "The Queen's Cloak." The queen has already had to give up her belief in fairy godmothers; now she must recognize that if anyone is going to help her, it will have to be herself. In her hour of need, no prince leaps to her rescue; no male figure rushes in to defend her. Where is her knight in shining armor when she needs him? Apparently, he does not exist.

After we reflect on the number of ways we have looked to men for help and protection, we find we must include other material. In addition to our real life experiences with men, we all carry a variety of male images within. Some are positive, others are negative but all represent aspects of our own personality which society and culture generally assign to men.

Carl Jung called these male archetypal figures a woman's animus. He made a few, unsuccessful attempts at defining its nature and effect, but he was much more able and interested in exploring the "feminine" side of a man's personality, which he called the anima.

Fortunately, male analysts have spent more time evaluating the female figures in their own psyches than speculating on what male figures do for women because, generally speaking, when it comes to the animus, I think most of their ideas are wrong. This is women's work, and various women analysts are now examining these multiple male figures which appear in our psyches.

There are only two significant animus figures in "The Queen's Cloak." Although this is hardly true of life, I will focus here on the characters that appear in this particular story. The first one is the thief, and unlike our experiences with the negative male in real life, sometimes the hostile acts of the psychic male can have positive consequences.

In order for the queen to continue her search for the centered self, she must abandon the idea that others will do the work for her. First, she must give up the magic mother. After her encounter with the wise woman, she reluctantly understands there is also no fairy godmother who will wave a magic wand. Finally, when she meets the thief, the queen is forced to recognize that salvation will never come from a prince or a millionaire.

How many times have we pinned our hopes on a man? How many times have we been disappointed? How many times have we stifled our own ideas, opinions, creativity, and energy because we thought we should wait for a man to take the initiative? He will guide us out of our perplexity or trouble into a better place. He will lead, we will follow. Our culture so persistently encourages us to think along these lines surely only a thief could rob us of this illusion.

His second contribution to the queen's development is equally important and feels equally devastating. He strips her naked, leaving her only the remnant of her mother's cloak. Although this aspect of the episode is very difficult, it is necessary. When the queen sets forth to meet her sister, she pulls out all the stops—she is regal to her toenails. She brings her best clothes and jewels, she brings presents. Yet all of these accoutrements are but a defense against her sister's power. Although all these fancy things make the queen feel secure, she cannot meet her sister while she is so well defended.

When we travel within our own psyches, particularly when we are in our sister's kingdom, we must be prepared to go naked. By taking everything she has, the thief precipitates the first of three occasions when the queen must be open and exposed. At this point, his actions force her to confront the negative mother. Unless he leaves the queen with nothing but the remnant of her mother's cloak, she would never look closely at those qualities and memories which she hates.

We know the queen has divided her mother's image into good and bad and kept the good parts for herself. Everything that was unpleasant about that relationship she plans to give her sister, whom she already detests. Her rejection of the bad mother is so complete, the queen even forgets to take that piece along on her trip. Fortunately, the maid remembers to tuck it among the royal packages. Now the thief has left her nothing but that "old rag."

Despite the fact that the thief's actions are instrumental in helping the queen prepare for her encounter with her sister, nothing must detract from the harrowing nature of this episode. He is not a good man in disguise, but despicable, like some men we have known in life. Let us be glad when he is finally gone.

Since there was nothing to do but continue,
she finally dragged the piece of cloak around
her. She was as sad and forlorn a figure as
any who ever trudged along the road.

Although easy to overlook, this episode actually marks one of the most important points of "The Queen's Cloak." It does not contain moments of high drama or derring-do that we have come to associate with myths and legends. Nor does it describe some heroic trial that tests the character of the hero.

This section seems so nondescript that many women in my workshops want to skip over it entirely. They are much more interested in the coming confrontation between the sisters than in these few transitional words. But if we pass over this episode too quickly, we will miss a deeply important interlude.

The significance of this passage is directly related to its subject. It marks the third time the queen must consider her relationship with her mother. We have seen her give up the magic mother; we stood by her side as she divided her cloak, rejoicing with her in happy memories of our own mother. We also watched the queen bundle up all the bad memories to forward to her sister. Never in her wildest dreams did the queen imagine she would have to bring those back to her heart and embrace them. But things do not always work out the way we plan. Now she is naked, without defense, and unable to avoid these disagreeable thoughts. How could any good come from this?

Needless to say, this is also one of my least favorite sections of the story. I am always reluctant to meditate on it, as are most women I know who have read "The Queen's Cloak." It is ironic that I am writing these words while sitting at my mother's desk. It is a formidable piece of furniture, the bottom half of an old, rolltop desk. When I was growing up, I came to know it very well. The drawers held paper, scissors, and glue; sometimes I could play with them. But the top of the desk, which always looked chaotic and was piled high with papers and pictures, was strictly out of bounds.

My mother was an editor, one of several on a New York bimonthly magazine. Later she was editor-in-chief of a smaller publication. She worked very hard and almost always brought home unfinished pages. I hated the sight of her heavy briefcase because I knew it meant she would have scant time for me.

After dinner, she would disappear into her study where she stayed until long after I went to bed. If I stood in the doorway, she would eventually look up in a distracted way. "Yes?" she would ask. If I interrupted her with a serious matter, she would stop and help me, but most of the time she would just sigh. "I know you can take care of that yourself," she'd say, and then she'd go back to work.

These are among my saddest memories. I resented my mother and her job, and my first inclination was to put these thoughts out of my mind. Who wants to dwell on such stuff or to notice later the corrosive effect their denial has on one's life? Only slowly did I come to realize I paid a high price for this strategy. In trying to be the perfect mother myself, I hesitated to start a career, and I never really talked with my mother about what she thought or felt during those years. What a waste! Now she is no longer alive, and all I can do is polish her desk, regret what I missed as a child, and grieve the shallow aspects of our adult relationship.

Because so much of one's unknown self is tied up with one's mother and influenced by her, even telling yourself "there are negative things about her but I don't want to think about them—yet" can seem very threatening. Certainly, when we get to this point in my workshops, the room is always very quiet.

Just as there are consequences for mild repression, there are major repercussions for more serious avoidance. Bad memories are difficult to work through, and most of us can only consider one or two without being in therapy or without some kind of group support. Nevertheless, the energy and options which we liberate in the process are reason enough to try.

Lifting up material she has repressed is a vital part of the queen's summer trip. She begins by recalling unhappy childhood memories of her mother. As dreadful as this experience may be, it helps prepare her for the second phase of this dark journey—the meeting with her sister.

In her relationship with her sister, the queen employed a different stratagem than she used with her mother. While she rejected any negative thoughts about her mother, she made her sister the dumping ground for all her own negative impulses. These projections allowed the queen to imagine it was not she who wanted to kill her sister but vice versa.

But now the game is up. Do you imagine the queen senses this as she trudges along the road? As the blows of summer continue to come, who cannot feel compassion for the queen? Hopefully you will feel some for yourself as you struggle with this difficult material. Better to try one small step, then move on to another episode. In my experience, every visit to this part of the fairy tale hurts, but each return is just a little easier to bear.

IV

*When she was ushered into the great hall, she
only had eyes for her sister. Gathering her
last strength, the woman removed the
remnant of their mother's cloak. Standing
naked, she offered it to her sister.
At that moment, she collapsed.*

"The time of the shadow" has come. With these words, Esther Harding announces one of the primary realities of mid-life (1975 p. 243). When she hands her sister the remnant, the queen acknowledges that she is ready to risk everything, including her life, in order to have her own cloak. This is danger indeed.

What could have brought her to this point? How different she seems from the passive, tentative, somewhat depressed woman we met at the beginning of "The Queen's Cloak." Working in the fields and challenging her husband and children seem to have made her stronger. Her encounter with the thief, even becoming acquainted with the negative aspects of her mother, have not deterred the queen. In fact, these earlier episodes appear to have made her more resolute. Now making the cloak means everything.

About twenty-five years ago, I first heard the wonderful Sumerian myth, "Inanna's Descent into the Underworld." It tells the story about the great goddess Inanna and her sister, Ereshkigal.

One day, for no apparent reason, Inanna announces she is going to visit her sister, the Queen of the Underworld. Since the Underworld is the land of the dead, Inanna knows she may not be able to return. If that happens, Inanna wants her steward to seek help from one of two gods. If neither of them will save her, Ninshubur should then go to Enki, the God of Wisdom, because surely he will not let Inanna die.

Having made these arrangements, the goddess knocks at the outer door of the Underworld and demands to see her sister. After consulting with Ereshkigal, the gatekeeper leads Inanna through the seven gates of the Underworld. At each one, he tells the goddess she must remove one of her royal garments. Finally, naked and bowed low, Inanna meets her sister.

> Then Ereshkigal fastened on Inanna
> the eye of death.
> She spoke against her the word of wrath.
> She uttered against her the cry of guilt.
> She struck her.
> Inanna was turned into a corpse,
> A piece of rotten meat,
> And was hung from a hook on the wall.
> (Wolkstein and Kramer 1983, p. 60)

When Inanna does not return after three days, Ninshubur goes to the gods for help. The first two refuse to save Inanna, but Enki is upset by what has happened to his daughter. He creates two creatures and, giving them the food and water of life, he sends them to the Underworld to rescue Inanna. After they bring her back to life, Inanna ascends to the land of the living, accompanied by a host of demons.

Twenty-five years ago, this is where the story ended. The ancient tablets recording the myth were either broken or missing, and scholars could only speculate on how it ended and why Inanna had made the journey. Now we have the entire story. But from the first time I read it, two things seemed clear: this is a woman's tale of death and resurrection; and Inanna went to visit her sister to become whole. For a woman who wants to know her centered self, the psychological wisdom of this myth remains unchanged.

The central motif of this episode of "The Queen's Cloak" describes a similar encounter, this time with one's shadow. The queen has come to her sister's realm in order to retrieve the evening shawl. Taking back various qualities she projected onto others is not a new experience for her, but now she needs to repossess her own dark side. The queen hates and fears this part of her being, as do we all. But she knows she must have the gifts of the shadow.

In the moment of their meeting, the queen gives up the last of her clothing to stand naked before her sister. This extraordinary gesture marks the high point, and the low point of the summer journey. The witching hour has come. Even though the queen feels death may be the result, she removes the last of her masks. This is the second time she glimpses her true self.

These highly dramatic events seem very far removed from our own lives, but as we reflect on this episode, we can appreciate certain similarities to our own experiences. Talking about our shadow and actually confronting the elements we have banished from our psyche are very different things. I believe the reality of the latter is much closer to the queen's ordeal than we might realize.

When I was a young woman, I climbed a mountain in Maine. From the top, one could see all of Mount Katahdin and the beautiful hills and valleys that rolled on to the horizon. Although I was with a friend who was an expert climber and very familiar with the area, I was terrified. I am basically a city mouse, so I could not even understand why it had become so important for me to be there. But something powerful seemed to draw me. Perhaps it was related to the mystical forces of Katahdin, which is Indian for "Great Spirit."

When we got above the tree line and first saw that magnificent vista, I had such a severe attack of vertigo that I thought I would fall off the mountain. But we kept going. In fact, we continued to climb along the rocky trail until the wind made my eyes tear so badly I couldn't see. This was the last straw, now I thought I would die.

I really like being in control of my life and my environment. Physical and psychological studies of men call this a type A personality. Most of the women I know are also type A; it is really important for them to be in charge of their own world, whether it is business, or family, or both. None of us like to rely on other people.

If you share this tendency, you will understand my level of discomfort. I was out of my element, I felt inept, I was truly scared. When my friend realized I was blinded, he told me to take his hand; he would lead me down the rocks to a place of shelter.

Although I was paralyzed with fear, I finally reached out my hand and let him talk me down the mountain and set me in the lee of a large rock. Looking back on that day, I know there was very little danger, and I doubt if my friend remembers the incident at all. But I will never forget it.

Since then I have taken other risks—spiritual and psychological ones—which seem equally hazardous. Rationally, I understand that something is in my best interest, but emotionally I may be unable to move. Faced with this impasse, it always takes a lot for me to let go of the old, established pattern to grasp the new. Reaching out to embrace the elements in one's shadow constitutes this kind of risk. It feels like death; we can only hope it brings new life.

V

*"We thought you might die. But we put our
resources at your disposal, and now you have
recovered."*

*Under the care of her sister, the woman
grew strong. They had time for many talks
and grew to know each other as never before.*

*"What can I give you to commemorate
our reunion then?"*
*"Many years ago, I made you a shawl
that resembled the starry night. Now I have
need of it. If you will give me that I will be
grateful."*
"It is yours," said her sister.

If the queen and Inanna are willing to face death to be reunited
with their dark sister, they must believe there is an important
reason to do so. In my opinion, becoming a whole person is a
more than adequate explanation for why they, or we, would
take this risk.

To a large extent, our culture and our families dictate
what is acceptable behavior for a woman. If we have any tendencies in the opposite direction, most of us disown them and
project them onto other people. We can then react with horror
at *their* behavior. This strategy allows us to feel virtuous but,
unfortunately, it alienates us from large parts of ourselves.

Each of us also has personal material we do not want to
acknowledge. These negative qualities are often pushed off on
all kinds of scapegoats. What a convenient system—until we
notice that as we give away more and more pieces of our being,
we have less and less access to ourselves. It is the same as trying

to adjust to some Procrustean bed; we just lop off those parts of ourselves that do not fit.

If only we could cut off our negative qualities by simply denying the shadow. But this figure also contains basic elements of a healthy personality that society has declared unacceptable in women. As a friend of mine commented, in the dark it is very difficult to separate these two categories, and it is debatable which characteristics are more offensive. Thus, when the queen reunites with her sister, she reestablishes contact with negative parts of her personality, but she also discovers positive qualities she did not realize she had. All these repressed attributes are gifts of the shadow and, surprisingly, they are what heal the queen.

Although every woman has her own list of characteristics she does not like, there are many similarities. For example, qualities like selfishness and aggressiveness can feel far more heinous than any of the seven deadly sins. Being thoughtless, competitive, unfeeling, unsupportive, opinionated, and petty may also seem just as terrible as jealousy, greed, arrogance, and hatred.

Our own personal biases create a second set of negative qualities. For type A people like me, for example, this includes being out of control and feeling weak or dependent.

Finally, there are attributes such as anger and sexuality which, despite recent changes in social mores, are still regarded as taboo. Indeed, direct access to these traits is so restricted that most of us continue to deny ourselves entrée to these powerful feelings.

Many of us retain the belief that negative feelings, such as anger at our husband or children, are not compatible with love. Many more of us are still embarrassed or repelled by our own sexual feelings. Even today, countless young women risk pregnancy rather than take responsibility for their own desires.

It is not a simple task to process all these various aspects of the shadow. Most of them arouse highly unpleasant feelings, if only because we judge ourselves so harshly; thus, it takes a long time to move from an intellectual understanding of these qualities to any true acceptance. The same material must be explored over and over before we stop projecting it onto our dark sister.

The struggle is worth it only because the gifts of the shadow are real. Through recognizing negative aspects of ourselves, we gain access to energy we have spent denying, repressing, or projecting unacceptable feelings and attributes.

Years ago, many of us were tyrannized by a psychological fad which encouraged us to "let it all hang out." If you felt it, do it; if you thought it, say it. This is not what I mean. I'm certainly not recommending we "act out" anything. In fact, I think that kind of behavior can be very self-destructive. The important thing is to know what we feel.

Having this information about ourselves can be extremely helpful. For example, a friend of mine became a private secretary to a corporate executive. Not long afterward, she began to get rather severe headaches and to have anxiety attacks. She knew she had a stressful job, but there was so much going on in her life at the time, she just kept plugging away.

After a year or so, my friend finally allowed herself to realize she hated her boss, whom she regarded as deceitful and manipulative. Once she recognized her feelings, and understood how angry she was, she promptly arranged a speedy transfer to another department. What had held her back was her self-image as a "Christian woman," which made it almost impossible for her to admit she could hate anyone. For over a year, she denied what she felt and suffered needlessly.

The more we know what we feel, the more choices we have. What we do with those options will vary from case to case. In my friend's situation, there was an easy, socially acceptable solution, and she took it. In other circumstances, we might decide to do nothing. But unless we make friends with our shadow, we will never have all the facts on which to base a decision.

Finally, this reunion with our sister also produces spiritual gifts. Too often, the bad angels floating around are none other than ourselves. Cut off from consciousness, our negative qualities easily become free-floating bogeys which terrify us. Perhaps the most important awareness, then, is that dualistic thinking cannot adequately describe our complicated lives. People cannot be neatly compartmentalized into good or bad. Neither can the queen.

Nothing is harder for me to give up than the idea of perfection. Perfect dinner parties, perfect books, perfect children, perfect me. Anything else is really not okay. Struggling to integrate the content of my shadow into my conscious life teaches me both the range and limitation of human nature.

Although I have reflected on these episodes many times, I know I will return to them again. Powerful feelings, both negative and positive, are hard to accept. Perhaps this is why the queen remains with her sister such a long time and does not request the midnight blue and silver shawl until the end of her lengthy visit. Even in this idealized story, only then is she ready to make the darkness part of her own cloak.

For this reason, when you reflect on this episode, have patience and care for yourself at least as well and as long as sister-shadow cared for the queen.

While she was relaxing, she noticed a man
coming down to the lake from the other side.
The woman concealed herself from view, but
continued to watch.
    Like herself, the man took off his clothes
and went for a swim.

The second major male figure in "The Queen's Cloak" is the
lover. What a different person! The thief stole everything from
the queen; the lover gives her something—the last bit of yarn
she needs to make her cloak.

Perhaps one of the reasons these two men are so un-
alike is because the queen is so different. When she sets off for
her sister's realm, the queen brings out her old persona. Hiding
behind her gifts, her fancy clothes, and her husband's power,
she tries to mask her fear and hostility.

On the way back, everything is different. The queen has
met the negative animus, traveled with her "bad" mother, stood
naked before her sister-shadow, and survived it all. More than
that, she has actually grown and changed. No wonder she does
not need a proud display to cover up her feelings. Now the
queen can travel simply and with confidence.

We sense her new assurance almost immediately. First,
she turns down her sister's offer of companionship. Despite her
earlier experience, she is not afraid of being alone. On the contrary, we can easily imagine that after all she has been through,
she might actually prefer to travel unaccompanied.

In addition to this act of courage, the queen displays an
ability to think for herself and to take other risks. Without consulting her ladies-in-waiting, her maid, or the wise woman, she
decides to go for a swim. Now the queen is pleased to take off
her clothes. This is the third time this season she has been naked, but what a contrast between this moment and the other two.

The differences between the queen's behavior in this episode and the others continue to amaze. Now she is hidden, her lover is exposed; she initiates their meeting, he responds; she is beautiful, he is appreciative. The queen discovers her own mind and acts for herself. No longer passive, she becomes animated and decisive as she seeks this encounter with her lover who, like the thief, represents part of herself.

For these reasons, it makes me sad that of all the episodes in "The Queen's Cloak," this is the only one which seems to offend anyone, the only one some women would like to see dropped from the story. Perhaps this is because the lover, like the thief, may be an actual person in your life either past, present, or future.

Certainly this reality can be very disconcerting, especially to women who are strictly monogamous in their own relationships. Women who have ruled out any possibility of being unfaithful often become very uncomfortable with the queen's behavior.

If this position reflects your own views, I hope you will focus on the fact that although the lover may represent a real man in some women's lives, he, like the thief, is an animus figure in every woman's psyche. Just as it is not necessary to get yourself mugged, it is not necessary to take a real-life lover in order to make your own cloak.

Who, then, is this animus lover, and what are his gifts to the queen? I believe he is the character who introduces the queen to her own sensuality and sexuality. Certainly our culture encourages us to repress this side of our nature. From the time we are young, we learn that good girls "just say no."

The exception to the rule is our pursuit of an "eligible" man, who will marry us and father our children. In recent years, I have had several conversations with different women who all indicated that they selected their husbands *primarily* because they thought they would be good fathers. Their expertise as lovers, their ability to excite and satisfy us, was far less important. Even the desire to find "a good provider" seems to take second place to an aspect of the maternal instinct I've rarely heard discussed.

Because sexuality can undercut this motive by being the "great complicator," our sensuality must be repressed. But as we get older and having babies becomes less likely or desirable, we may discover aspects of ourselves we did not expect. Suddenly we may want to say yes to our own sexual desire. When this happens, the animus lover can help us by drawing us out of our restrictive little worlds.

Beyond this obvious correlation, the lover also puts us in touch with all aspects of our senses. Do you suddenly remember you always wanted to paint or sculpt? Or write detective stories or be a poet? Are you suddenly inspired to do something wonderfully different or something daring that would test your limits? Do you want to go back to school or start a business?

Any and all of these enterprises can be inspired and encouraged by this lover. Because our senses key us into our own genuine possibilities, they ground us in the real world. The queen has not been aware of her ability to evaluate reality and to dream dreams she can make come true. Now she knows she can act wisely on her own behalf.

When the queen realizes that the animus lover is the stranger the wise woman said she must find, she happily asks him for his leggings. Their earth tones will now become part of her cloak, reminding her of the way feet touch the ground and that she has something to stand on. No wonder that whenever I want to evaluate something, make a major professional decision, or take a risk, I willingly reflect on this episode. It is my animus lover who helps me to know and trust my own judgment and experience.

This lovely interlude ends the difficult summer months with a healing experience. Both her encounter with the woodsman and her purifying swim refresh her body and soul. Now she is prepared to reenter her realm and undertake the trials of the last season.

FALL

I

*The Queen tried to remember the pattern in
her mother's cloak. I wish I had not unraveled
it so quickly, she thought. But she did recall
patches of blue from the piece she clutched to
her body as she stumbled to her sister's castle.
I do not have any blue, she thought, except for
a few strands, so I will dye the flax that color
in memory of her.*

After several years of reflecting on various episodes from "The
Queen's Cloak," I have discovered that each season appears to
have its own general motif. Winter is one of personal evaluation. Unraveling and changing intimate relationships dominates
the spring. Summer finds the queen struggling with negative
or unknown material within herself.

The prevailing mood of autumn is reconciliation. In
various ways and at different times, we watch the queen re-
sume her relationships with family and friends. By the end of
the season, she even reconnects with the wider community.
Nevertheless, because the queen has changed so much, these
relationships are not the same. Her own transformation alters
everything.

The first, and one of the more dramatic indications of
her different nature, appears in this episode. As in each previ-
ous season, the queen spends some of her time examining the
relationship with her mother. In winter she gave up the magic
mother; during spring and summer, she considered the good
and the bad parts of their relationship. Now she yearns to recall
the whole person and recognize her mother's influence on her life.

In this episode, the mother the queen decides to honor is not some patched-up character made of assorted memories from the past. Now an entirely new figure has emerged. Thus, when I reflect on this passage, I don't alternate my thoughts between chocolate chip cookies and the times my mother was too busy for me; rather I find myself discovering a whole woman I hardly know. Each time I come back to this section, I find a different image. I see her as though through a kaleidoscope and watch the complex pattern of her life shift and shift again. Sometimes the darker colors predominate, others times the light, but the design and the colors are always mixed in surprisingly complex ways. It has become clear, at last, that it is not possible to separate "good" mother from "bad" mother without destroying the true person. Here is my mother—finally a whole, real woman, her self.

This reconnection with one's mother is not based on fantasy, naive appreciation, or anger. On the contrary, it emerges out of a profound awareness of the complexity of human personality and a respect for the integrity of her life. Now that the queen has assembled all her own bits of yarn, she can begin to understand some of the diversity represented by the pattern in her mother's cloak.

Perhaps she also recognizes that the more she integrates the image of her mother, the more she can integrate herself. Because Western culture constantly bombards us with dualistic images of women, keeping the full spectrum of one's mother's attributes together is very difficult. Nevertheless, I believe this effort holds the key to seeing ourselves as whole people. If our image of the woman most influential in our lives is hopelessly fragmented, how can we hope to get ourselves "together"?

At this point, the queen regrets her hasty decision to cut up her mother's cloak, "as many of us do when we start the process," added a friend. Although she can no longer talk with her mother or study her design, the queen is determined to honor their relationship in some substantial way. Her mother's influence on her life has been so profound that she wants to acknowledge their closeness. Simply adding the few threads from her mother's cloak won't do.

In the introduction, I mentioned the game of three-dimensional tic-tac-toe, using it as a metaphor to describe various levels in our lives and how they interrelate. Although most of us concentrate on only one or two planes, we can explore all of them whenever we wish. Under the circumstances, it is not surprising that the more we reach out for wholeness, the more we need to examine all our own various aspects.

During these final months, the queen begins to explore what I call the spiritual dimension of her life which, although always present, may not always be as evident as the personal, familial, and cultural levels. Our desire to bring together the disparate parts of our lives and to integrate them into some universal frame has evoked the spiritual yearnings of people throughout the ages. For this reason, we should not be surprised that when the queen seeks to unify her life, she connects with this deeper layer of her self.

It is the queen's decision to dye the flax blue "in memory of her," which signals the queen's ability to see beyond her individual mother into the spiritual dimension. The whole mother, who we celebrate in this passage, may be the one who connects us to female figures associated with the divine or representative of the holy. For some people, an obvious example of such a figure is the Virgin Mary. She has long been identified with the color blue: it is the traditional shade of her cloak. Blue is also a symbol of sea and sky, peace and purity.

But the Virgin celebrated in Christianity has sisters and predecessors in other traditions. Although Athena, Diana, and other goddesses from the Hellenistic world are familiar figures, almost every age and culture has worshiped some feminine representation of the Holy. These goddesses were also called Virgin. Their sexual innocence, or lack of it, was not the issue. They were Virgins because they were in control of their own lives and not under the dominion of their father, husband, son, or other male relative.

Artemis and Isis, often singled out as foremothers of Mary, illustrate this independent nature very clearly. Neither the chastity of one nor the wedded status of the other affect their title. For them, as well as for Aphrodite, Inanna, and Cybele, being Virgin simply means being One-In-Themselves.

In recent years, many women have discovered goddess figures. Some find them to be lively, viable alternatives to the male images of the divine prevalent in Judaism and Christianity. Some women, like Nelle Morton, have discovered divine female images within their own psyches. But even those of us who have not connected to these symbols sense that this remarkable designation, "Virgin," has implications for our own spirituality. We may not yet understand how that might be, but at a deep level we understand that divine female figures might open up a bridge to female wholeness, female individuation, and our centered selves.

No wonder we are not surprised that it is our desire to honor our "whole" mother that draws us beyond her into a deeper spiritual level where women figures are holy and one-in-themselves. Our mother is not the same as a male anima creature who, like Dante's Beatrice, inspires and leads him through Paradise. Nor is she a mysterious, alien creature who inhabits the nether regions. Our mother is related to us, bone of our bone and flesh of our flesh. She is always grounded in the physical and personal aspects of our relationship, and we never lose the memories connected with them, but at this point in our reflections, we begin to connect with a new image and allow it to join the others.

Today the queen has opened a new door to her self, and we can sense her deeper understanding.

The more she thought about this project, the
harder it became. As she planned, she tried to
imagine how it would appear to others.
    Will it look regal? Will it make me look
strong, she thought? What is the best style?
How can I work in all the patterns and
colors?
    As the days grew shorter, the Queen
became more upset. No one could help her,
and she began to feel that all her work had
been in vain.

If we have any doubt that personal, social, and cultural factors continue to shape and reshape our lives, this episode forcefully reminds us of their continuing influence. The wonderful moment of integration and appreciation, which opens up new aspects of spirituality for the queen, is over. Now she must focus on her last major task. For me, it is always one of the hardest.

Commenting on the queen's struggle, one of my students observed that "having all the pieces and putting them together are not the same thing." Clearly, this is the case. The queen has assembled all the elements of her cloak; now the only remaining hurdle is to design it to please herself. Why should this be so difficult?

Originally, this part of the wise woman's instructions seemed to be the easiest. Now it appears to be the rock that will break her to bits. And the harder she tries, the worse everything gets.

When I contemplate this episode, I often recall the story about Sambo and the tigers who steal his clothes. Each one takes something, but soon each covets what the other has. Eventually, they begin to chase each other around a big tree. Faster and faster they run until all three of them dissolve in a heap of tiger butter. Then Sambo returns, picks up his clothes, and goes home.

My frustration with this final task often makes me feel like the tigers. I have chased "solutions," which seemed almost within my grasp, but I have yet to discover a trick or a formula which can make this last labor easy.

Whenever I contemplate designing my own cloak, I run into the rock of family, social, and cultural pressure which tells me who I am, what I ought to be, and how I ought to think and feel. I become intensely aware that the primary message assaulting me from every direction is that a woman is a person for others, that she is not really complete without an "other." In other words, the very idea that a woman could be one-in-herself becomes a contradiction in terms.

My women friends and I often discuss this dilemma. All of us give lip service to the idea of independence and self-actualizing, but in daily life we know we compromise away the reality—a little bit here, a little bit there. In the end, most of our focus remains on the other.

It seems that no sooner do we glimpse the possibility of wholeness, of being one-in-ourselves, than we become conscious of all the demands on our integrity. Every "should" and "ought" concerning our behavior and self-understanding appears to rise up and call our name.

Unfortunately, these forces assailing us are not only the semiabstract "powers and principalities" of society, our social and political leaders, and our cultural norms. They are also our parents, siblings, spouses, children, employers, friends, professors, and pastors. All of them have opinions about who we are or ought to be, and trying to please them all can turn us into tiger butter.

Beyond these traditional, often self-serving images, are the projects we want to finish and the jobs we enjoy. But even the people we love may turn into monsters. Members of our families, our therapists, our best friends can become some of those demons because anyone and everyone who has a plan for us becomes part of the problem.

At this moment in "The Queen's Cloak" many of us become acutely conscious of these personal and social expectations. Even the spring task of reclaiming what we have projected onto others may seem easy in comparison. Once the goal of making our own cloak seemed within our grasp, now it slips beyond reach. And no one can help us—no wise woman or maid, no friendly animal, dwarf, prince charming, or fairy godmother can design our own cloak. We have only our selves, all our balls of yarn, and our misguided notion that somehow we can get the pattern to come out "right."

Who cannot share the queen's frustration and her growing anxiety?

One day, she sat down on the floor and placed
the balls of yarn around her.

From where I sit, she thought, some colors
seem more complimentary than others. And
so she moved the balls around her. While she
did, she held them in her hand, gathering in
her lap those she was unsure about until she
found the perfect place.
    That afternoon, she played until she
knew all the shades and textures of her yarn.
Finally the Queen had them spread about her
in a way that pleased her. Even the colors she
didn't like had found a place.
    Then she stood up in the middle of
them. At that moment, she knew how to
design her cloak. The cloak flows out from me,
she thought. The colors and patterns will
only look right when they come out from the
center. "Which is me," she said out loud with
a smile and a tremble.

Writing about this episode in "The Queen's Cloak" is very difficult. I cannot give you a plan or any suggestion on how to do
what the queen does. Even if I could, I would just become part
of the problem—like those friends who say "if you'd only stop
worrying about this."
    Although this demur is true, another reason why I find
this passage so hard to describe is because I have so much to
learn about the queen's capacity to be centered. When I was in
high school, we used to have a May Day celebration. It was one
of those quasi-medieval events complete with court and queen.

Twice I got to dance the Maypole. Holding one of the ribbons, I would join the others weaving in and out until the pole was wrapped. This is a process I understand. Knowing what it feels like to be the Maypole is what eludes me. Yet this centeredness is what the queen discovers.

To know you are the Maypole is to know yourself profoundly connected to all aspects of your life from the most spiritual to the most trivial. This knowledge omits nothing—not one's desire for wholeness, one's fits of temper, one's inability to keep up a correspondence, or the premenstrual pimple on one's cheek. The centered self the queen discovers includes all this.

At this moment, the queen also understands that she is more than the sum of her obvious parts. When she stands up, she senses the powerful connection which runs through her to the earth and to the divine. Some traditions call this the *axis mundi.* Or perhaps this experience is similar to that moment when Buddha's hand touched the ground and he became enlightened. No wonder the discovery makes her tremble.

There have been fleeting moments in my life, and in the lives of women I know, that have produced this awed sense of joy. I always try to hang onto these flashes of awareness, but they never last. So I return to meditate my way through "The Queen's Cloak" over and over again.

When I do, I often think about the queen sitting on the floor, moving the balls of yarn around her, holding each one in her lap until she finds its proper place. In the metaphor of the fairy tale, these balls represent various attributes of the queen's nature. Since many of them were repressed, projected, or unknown, her first responsibility was to gather them together. Now, as she holds the various yarns in her hands and lap, she comes to know them.

The difference between these two levels of awareness, the gathering and the knowing, is huge. Whenever we say "I know . . . BUT," we are still trying to minimize or ignore aspects of ourselves we do not like. However, when the queen places all the balls in her lap and then arranges them around her, she does something very rare—she agrees to know and accept her self as she is that very minute.

When I reflect on this episode, I fantasize the queen sitting on the floor. She picks up a ball of yarn from her sister's cloak, says "Yuck," and throws it across the room. Soon other balls are sent flying until there are only a few left in front of her. "Good," says the queen, contentedly, until she spies one of the rejected missiles. "Hmmmm, maybe that wouldn't look bad over here."

Before she knows it, she is crawling around the floor retrieving balls from the corners, from under the bureau, from on top of the chair. Soon she has a lap full of odds and ends. Maybe she worries some in her fingers like beads, or squashes them between her hands. Others she may set aside time and time again before she finds a place where they will *add* to the pattern which is slowly evolving.

Obviously, this royal game takes a great deal of time. Because this is a fairy tale, the queen does it all in one afternoon; in reality, this task may take longer than all the rest combined. Thus, each time I return to this passage, I usually focus on only one or two personal qualities, trying to understand how they fit in my life, how they contribute to the design of my cloak. It is because each attribute is part of me and nothing can be rejected, that this task takes such a long time.

One sustaining grace derives from the element of spirituality the queen discovered earlier. Although this spiritual dimension has many aspects, the work of psychoanalyst D. W. Winnicott suggests an image that can comfort and encourage us at this difficult time (1965, p. 17).

When we were small most of us had a "good enough" mother. Sitting in her lap, we experienced the security of her arms around us, we felt safe. As we get older, the size of that lap gradually expands until, figuratively speaking, it can include the room, the house, the neighborhood, the whole town. In that space, that holding space bounded by the mother's arms, we are able to play creatively, totally confident of our safety.

Most of us lose the sense of this space as we grow up, and some of us have never known it at all, but I believe the queen enters such a place. Because designing one's own cloak is a creative act which can only be carried out in a similar atmosphere of safety and approval, I imagine that at this moment the queen experiences the divine as a type of safely bounded lap. The space within is left for her to fill with her Self.

Many years ago, I had a split-second epiphany. I was talking with a friend when suddenly I felt the room fill with a divine presence which took up every corner, every inch. First I was overwhelmed, but then I felt a compelling sense of hospitality. Later, as the presence began to recede, I felt invited to live into that emptying space. Indeed, it was only when the divine presence withdrew that there was room for me to be.

Because this experience of the divine had no image, no sex, no creedal dimensions, it took me more than twenty-five years to find the words and a concept which could begin to describe such a strange encounter. Without some kind of context, it was even hard for me to take it seriously.

During the years after my experience, I found myself growing increasingly critical of established Christian images, so I decided to study theology. When the feminist protest appeared, and recovery of the female and feminine dimensions of the divine became more possible, I was delighted to add my voice.

Although I cherish many of these insights, I have slowly come to realize that they do not actually illuminate my own experience. Only Nelle Morton's description of the divine as One who "hears us to speech" captures any of the divine quality I felt, momentarily, so long ago (1985, p. 129). She interprets the Divine Silence as a way the Holy One invites us to speak our own words and, therefore, to know our own selves.

In a similar way, I believe the absence of god, the emptiness many of us experience, actually creates a spiritual space we are invited to fill with our own being. Because the Divine is still present at the boundaries of this space, at the circumference, this emptiness becomes a safe, holding space, a Holy Lap we can move into when we lay out the pattern of our cloaks.

When the queen enters into this holy, empty space she can be confident she has the room, the time and permission to explore every aspect of herself. With every duality accepted, good and bad, she can just be herself. When she discovers that self is part of the Holy One and a unique cocreator with the divine, like Sophia and Miriam, I imagine the queen dances with joy.

Finally the Queen and her maid set up the loom. As the Queen began to weave, she started to sing. They had a merry time, and soon everyone in the castle found reasons to come to the Queen's apartments.

These words signal the start of the final reconciliations. As a woman becomes more grounded in her centered self, more open to her energy and experiences, she becomes a magnet for everyone around her. Because she is more joyful and content in her own self, she begins to exude a genuine happiness that everyone finds attractive. Who would not want to be with her? Spiritually, intellectually, and sensually, she is more alive than ever before; no wonder the king comes "more than most."

What a contrast! The queen is no longer passive, dependent, or depressed. She does not need others to carry feelings and attributes she wants to deny or is afraid to accept. Nor has she become a narcissistic, self-centered person. Rather, her inward work has made her self-aware, and now the queen begins to reconnect with her family and friends in a much more positive way.

"Now it is time to go back to see the wise woman," said the Queen.

"Do you want me to tell you about the magic?"
"No," said the Queen. "I understand. It is not in the cloak. That is why you could not tell me. It comes from making the cloak."
"Yes," said the wise woman as she stood up, "I see you have become a wise woman yourself."
The two women laughed and embraced. They spent the day enjoying each other's company, stringing garlands for the winter festival, and eating and drinking cakes and wine.

The reestablishment of her relationships eventually leads the Queen to return to the wise woman's door. This time she is neither imperious nor timid. Now that she has made her own cloak, there is no one to defy and nothing to hide. There is only one piece of information left to disclose. Working on the cloak has drawn everyone toward her. Is it really magic after all?

"No," says the queen, with conviction. She knows there is no power or magic in the cloak. Her strength, authority, and potency derive from what she has done and what she has learned about her self working alone and with others. It also stems from her encounter with the divine. The cloak is only a momentary expression of a long and complex process.

It may be distressing to know that the design the queen creates that happy afternoon only captures a moment in her life. Because she will change and change again, she could create hundreds of different patterns. And each one would be different. Only a fairy tale makes this event seem static and final. In real life, we learn more about ourselves each time we consider the episodes of "The Queen's Cloak." Every time we meditate on them we will find something new, so the patterns in our cloak will vary. We can always discover something startling about ourselves, something we never expected, but once we have felt ourselves to be centered like the Maypole, our return to the tasks ceases to be a labor of Sisyphus.

Now we go back over the various passages of "The Queen's Cloak" to enlarge our self-awareness, to please ourselves, to know our selves better—not to find our self. We will still know frustration, anger, and sorrow but the not-so-quiet desperation that shades much of the queen's early journey is no longer present.

Earlier in the fairy tale, the queen wisely chose her maid as a life companion. In this episode, she establishes a similar relationship with the wise woman. Because becoming self-aware is an ongoing adventure, it is important to keep company with someone who knows the journey and who can help you stay on track.

As she did with her maid, the queen celebrates her choice of companion by sharing food. This simple act seems to have universal meaning as a symbol of friendship and hospitality. In many traditions, it also has spiritual significance, and through the years I have met many women seminary students who want to be ordained so they can preside over such a communion table. The picnic shared by the queen and her maid and the cakes and wine eaten with the wise woman evoke these spiritual meals. But rather than commemorate the sacrificial atonement of Jesus, they celebrate the hospitality of the divine which we can show one another.

Anyone can preside over this sacred table as long as the meal is shared.

And the Queen used her wisdom like magic
to bring peace and healing to the land.

Most fairy tales conclude with the phrase "and they lived happily ever after," but these words are inappropriate for "The Queen's Cloak." This story ends by reconnecting the queen with her family and friends, and by her choice of the wise woman as another life companion. But it also points to her greater involvement with an even wider group. A transformed woman will gradually move beyond her immediate circle and connect with the world, where she will share the gifts of her spirit.

In the summer section, I mentioned a woman who recognized her anger and left an employer she hated. Those were hard years for her. There were family crises with children and aging parents, as well as difficulties with her husband. Throughout this time, she continued to attend church and to serve as a nominal member of several committees. She had always done that, but in those days she would occasionally tell me she thought the church had grown remote, detached from those people it most needed to help. Then, as now, she spoke for many as well as herself.

Then gradually she began to change. This unassuming, unpretentious woman began to take the initiative. She started to speak up at meetings and to take stands on controversial issues. She became an advocate for the homeless and an organizer for the local food pantry. Her visits to the sick were not social calls; she would help them get dressed, drive them to the doctor, do their laundry. Where death had come, whether from cancer or AIDS, she would offer gentle and competent hands to do what needed to be done.

Within five years, without any fanfare at all, she had became a major force in her church and widely respected in her community. To this day, she occasionally wonders if she can take on a new issue, start up a controversial program, or speak at a large meeting. Then, expressing her nervousness and voicing her inadequacies, she just does it.

Although I know little about her internal struggles, no one can miss the radical change in her outward behavior. I do not know what caused it, but the results are dramatic. Fifteen years ago she was a rather nondescript woman who apologized for almost everything. Today she radiates a remarkable contentment. She seems happy and quite well aware of her feelings, capabilities, and limitations. You might still walk by her on the street, but if you spoke with her at any length, you might sense being in the presence of a wise woman.

She will laugh when she reads this and be very embarrassed, but I think she is like the queen. She is not glamorous or rich, she is just an ordinary woman like most of us. Yet she has an integrity and a wholeness about her which is definitely not ordinary, and she inspires me all the time.

During these last episodes, the queen has come to know herself as centered in the universe with access to all the various dimensions of her life. Because she lives an abundant life, she is inspired to share her gifts and talents with others. Indeed, her generosity and consideration are as much a hallmark of the individuated life as her self-awareness and centeredness.

Because her "doing" flows from within, like water bubbling up from a natural spring, the queen does not exhaust herself caring for others. On the other hand, neither could she imagine withholding her particular gifts from the world. Because the queen's quest is not a narcissistic search for "self-fulfillment" nor an exercise in "self-aggrandizement," the queen is able to be more open and affirming of others as well as her self.

This giving response clearly indicates that "The Queen's Cloak" cannot end in an orgy of self-congratulation. Knowing ourselves as centered within and without, and experiencing ourselves as a type of Maypole that anchors us in both the human and the divine, continually transforms our lives. The balance, humor, and dependability that characterize the queen's personal relationships and inspire her social commitments are among the surest signs of her wisdom. Taking time to make and remake our own cloak is what keeps us in touch with who we really are and what matters in our lives.

WORKS CITED

Bass, Ellen, and Laura Davis. 1988. *The Courage to Heal*. New York: Harper and Row.

Downing, Christine. 1987. *Journey Through Menopause: A Personal Rite of Passage*. New York: Crossroad.

Harding, M. Esther. 1975. *The Way of All Women*. New York: Harper Colophon Books.

Jung, Carl. 1951. *Aion. CW*, vol. 9ii. Princeton, N.J.: Princeton University Press, 1959.

Morton, Nelle. 1985. *The Journey Is Home*. Boston: Beacon Press.

Shange, Ntozake. 1975. *for colored girls who have considered suicide/when the rainbow is enuf*. New York: Bantam Books.

Winnicott, D. W. 1965. *The Family and Individual Development*. London: Tavistock Publications.

Wolkstein, Diane, and Samuel Noah Kramer. 1983. *Inanna: Queen of Heaven and Earth*. New York: Harper and Row.

INDEX

violence, 31
Virgin Mary, 95

whole woman, 93-94
wholeness, 59, 67, 86, 95-96, 98,
    101, 109
Winnicott, D. W., 102
wisdom, 110
wise man, 45
wise woman, 29, 44-47, 54,
    56-60, 66, 69, 72, 74, 77, 90, 92,
    97, 99, 106-108